SUCCESS in SHORT SALES

A Step-By-Step Guide to Success in
Pre-Foreclosure Short Sales for Residential Agents

BY

LONI PARMELLY

Wilshire-Remington* Publishing Company
Dallas, Texas
First Edition 2004

SUCCESS IN SHORT SALES (formally known as "Pre-Foreclosure Short Sales for Residential Agents"). Copyright © 2004 Registration Number TXU 1-161-363. Manufactured in the United States of America. All rights reserved. **No part of this book may be reproduced in any form or by any electronic or mechanical means including information storage and retrieval systems without permission in writing from the publisher, except by a reviewer, who may quote brief passages in a review.** Published by Wilshire-Remington* Publishing Company, P. O. Box 182184, Arlington, Texas 76096. (877)210-6269 toll free. Fax # (347) 521-5560. First edition.

Visit our website at **www.SSQConsulting.com** for more information on Short Sales and Consulting Services for Residential Real Estate Agents and Brokers.

ISBN # 0-9754580-3-5

Edited by Linda Coy-Bailey, Amanda Petrovskiy, Jarrod Parmelly, and Robert J. Dyer

DEDICATION

This book is dedicated to my Children, Amanda and Jarrod. They have encouraged me to follow my dreams, as I have encouraged them to follow theirs. And, to my late husband, Bill, who made me the woman, I am today. Without the love and devotion of my family and friends, the trip here would not have been as pleasant. And, finally, this book is dedicated to all the Loss Mitigators whose hard work and creativity has given Investors, Agents, and Sellers the opportunity to make the World a better place.

The following Investors are named in this book: Federal National Mortgage Association or Fannie Mae, Federal Home Loan Mortgage Corporation or Freddie Mac, Veteran's Association or VA, US Department of Housing and Urban Development or HUD, Federal Housing Association or FHA, and Resolution Trust Corporation or RTC. This in no way constitutes their individual opinions, permissions, or consents to this work.

Although the Author and Publisher have exhaustively researched all sources to ensure accuracy and completeness of the information contained in this book, we assume no responsibility for errors, inaccuracies, omissions or any other inconsistency herein. Any slights against people or organizations are unintentional. Readers should consult an attorney or accountant for specific application to their individual State or County regulations and restrictions. The information in this book is taken from twelve years of experience, and reflects the opinion of the Author.

Attention Colleges, Universities, Corporations, Writing and Publishing organizations: Quantity discounts are available on bulk purchases of this book for Educational Training purposes, Fund-Raising, or gift giving. Special books, booklets, or book excerpts can also be created to fit your specific needs. For more information contact SSQ Consulting Company, Bulk Sales, P.O. Box 182184, Arlington, Texas 76096, toll free (877)210-6269, or fax (347)521-5560.

ACKNOWLEDGEMENTS

Thanks to all my family and friends, who encouraged me to pursue my dream of contributing something to this world. I also want to express my gratitude to Dawn and Chad at ADP Media Group in Fort Worth, Texas. And, to friends Linda Coy-Bailey, Kristi Lorance, and Melda Cruz for their contributions to this work. I also want to give a heart felt Thanks to Dr. George Blumenschein, Patty Decker, and the entire staff at the Arlington Cancer Center. For without their expert care, I would not have had the chance to pursue "Chapter Two" of my life.

OTHER UPCOMING PROJECTS

SELLER'S SHORT SALE HANDBOOK

This booklet will explain the Seller's benefits for participating in the Investor's pre-foreclosure Short Sale option. The Seller will be taken step by step through the financial package preparation and financial documentation requirements. Most common questions/answers will fully inform the Seller and help the Agent save time and money. This affordable booklet encourages the Seller to complete the information for the Investor accurately and completely. It can be bought individually or in bulk and included in the financial package or sent as a follow up to the Agent's initial contact. The booklet can be utilized by Investors, Servicers, MI Companies, Credit Counseling Agencies, and the entire Real Estate Community.

MY ATTORNEY HAS QUESTIONS

This, affordable, booklet will come in handy as a follow up to the Seller's Short Sale Handbook when their Attorney has specific questions. This booklet is sold individually, or in bulk, and will be a question/answer series. The booklet will be co-written with Attorneys to assure their scope of questions are answered accurately.

FORMS CD

This CD will include the financial statements used by all Investors, MI Companies and most Second liens. Copies of the breach letter, financial documentation requirements, and State foreclosure statutes. The CD will be instrumental in preparing Pre-Foreclosure Short Sale packages for Sellers who desire to participate in selling their homes for less than owed. Special tips and suggestions will help both Agents and Sellers. Microsoft Word, Excel and Acrobat programs required. This CD is a must have. A clean copy every time!

CONTACT US: **SSQ Consulting Company**
P.O. Box 182184
Arlington, Texas 76096
(877)210-6269 toll free
Fax: (347)521-5560

SSQConsulting@Yahoo.com
www.SSQConsulting.com

TABLE OF CONTENTS

Chapter One - What is a Short Sale?	Page	1
Chapter Two - The Players	Page	5
Chapter Three - A Little Short Sale History	Page	9
Chapter Four - My Sellers Don't Understand	Page	15
Chapter Five - Getting Started	Page	23
Foreclosure Time Table	Page	26
Chapter Six - Listing a Short Sale	Page	33
Chapter Seven - Fair Market Value	Page	41
Chapter Eight - Environmental Issues	Page	49
Chapter Nine - Second Liens	Page	57
Chapter Ten - What is the MI Company?	Page	63
Chapter Eleven - My Seller Has Filed Bankruptcy	Page	69
Chapter Twelve - My Seller is Deceased	Page	75
Chapter Thirteen - The Short Sale Offer	Page	79
Chapter Fourteen - Contingencies, and Other Contract Requirements	Page	87
Chapter Fifteen - Negotiation Pointers	Page	91
Chapter Sixteen - Closing a Short Sale	Page	97
Chapter Seventeen - Short Sale Scenarios	Page	103
Chapter Eighteen - Seller's Short Sale Benefit Review	Page	113
Forms Seller's Authorization Form	Page	120
Forms Seller's Questionnaire Form	Page	121
Forms Loss Mitigation Document Requirements	Page	123
Forms Seller's Financial Statement	Page	124
Forms Seller's Hardship Letter	Page	125
Glossary of Terms	Page	126
Index	Page	131
Order Form	Page	134

Chapter One

WHAT IS A SHORT SALE??

Pre-Foreclosure Short Sales are more commonly known as "Short Sales", and they are quickly becoming the newest Specialization in Real Estate. But, what *is* a Short Sale? A Pre-Foreclosure Short Sale is simply what it looks like; homes sold "prior" to the foreclosure sale, and "short" of a full payoff. Short Sale candidates have negative equity, and are experiencing financial hardship. Real Estate Agents no longer have to market homes at unreasonable list prices due to the remaining balance on the mortgage! You can list Short Sales for fair market value.

Short Sales are mortgage loans in jeopardy of foreclosing. They are homes of Sellers who no longer have the ability to make their mortgage payments and want to sell the home. National foreclosure rates directly affect the demand for the Short Sale. Well, the demand is there! Just imagine having the opportunity to list, and close, every foreclosure in your County. The knowledge you receive from this little book will give you the guidance you need to increase your listings and commissions drastically. Learn a Short Sale process that **REALLY** works!

Investors, like Fannie Mae, Freddie Mac, FHA and VA, save millions of dollars per year by approving Short Sales, instead of taking the property back after foreclosure, and placing it on the market as an REO (Real

Estate Owned) property. Investors agree that the Short Sale generates higher "Savings Over REO" over their other "alternatives to foreclosure" options. Other options offered to delinquent Sellers revolve around their ability to keep the property. But, not all Sellers have this ability, with unemployment rates remaining steadily high.

Investors are eager to work hand in hand with the Real Estate Community in an attempt to help Sellers avoid unnecessary credit damage in this struggling economy. The Investor can reduce their potential losses by selling the home *prior* to foreclosure, and they guarantee your commission! "For Sale By Owner" listings can now be a reality since many "FSBO's" are actually Short Sales. To understand why the Investor would want to do Short Sales, you have to put yourself in their position. It's all business.

When a mortgage loan is delinquent, it accrues additional daily expenses like delinquent interest and escrows. This can increase the payoff so high, the fair market value of the asset will not pay off the loan. The Investor incurs a loss at this point, whether they choose to foreclose, or sell it as a Short Sale. Of course, if the Investor chooses to foreclose, they can pursue a judgment (in some states), place a foreclosure on the credit report, and, in most cases, file a 1099 showing capital gains for the Seller. The Short Sale relieves the Seller from these credit damaging factors.

As previously mentioned, Investors offer additional options to Sellers who wish to keep their home. However, they must qualify financially and/or pay a large portion of the delinquency to retain ownership. These options are modifications, repayment, or forbearance plans. The Pre-Foreclosure Short Sale option allows the Seller to sell the home for less than a full payoff. So although the Investor incurs a definite loss, it can be substantially less than they would lose with a foreclosed property. Because of this, the Investor offers specific benefits for the Seller for participating in the Short Sale option. FHA will even pay the Seller $750 at closing! With increasing foreclosure rates across the Nation, Investors are making the Short Sale process more streamlined all the time.

You may have heard horror stories about how long the Short Sale takes, frustrating countering, and commission adjustments. There are solutions to most of these problems. What is so spectacular about the Short Sale is *EVERYONE* benefits. The Investor, the Servicer, the Mortgage Insurance Company, and yes; the Residential Agent, all walk away from the closing in a Win-Win position. If you could avoid all the above concerns, and net a guaranteed commission in record time, would it peak your interest? Of course it would!

First, get organized with the proper forms, knowledge, and resources available in this book. You will learn how to avoid many of the pitfalls plaguing the Short Sale process. Most Servicers are now fully staffed with Loss Mitigation Departments, giving Real Estate Agents an opportunity to obtain the Investor's approval on Short Sales much quicker. Since the length of the Short Sale process has steadily been tightened over the past few years, the entire approval process now takes as little as 1-2 weeks. That is exceptional compared to the early days of the Short Sale when few processes were in place for approvals. This information has never been readily available to Agents, until now. This book is designed to aid Licensed Residential Real Estate Agents, and their Brokers, reach Short Sale goals by taking you through the process step-by-step, or chapter by chapter.

Second, if you have the ability to set the listing price at fair market value from the onset, you can avoid months and months of fruitless marketing (sometimes at your own expense). Avoid accepting offers too low to consider due to underestimating the value. Once the Investor's value is received, you will be able to set the list price at fair market value. The most efficient approach to the Short Sale, is to start from the beginning; with the listing. Use the *Seller's Questionnaire* in *Forms* to help determine the payoff position of the loan and the possible need for a Short Sale.

And, third, you will learn how to cut the listing time down to 3 months on most homes. Because the listing price is set by the Investor, based on their fair market value, the offers will start to roll in. No more unproductive listings. Three to six month listings are normal on Short Sales. FHA (Federal Housing Association) will even pay the Seller an additional $250 for closing within 3 months! That is a total of $1,000 in FHA benefits for the Seller of a Short Sale.

Foreclosures have increased all over the Country – It seems like economically, there have been few improvements since the mid 1980's. Homes in the United States are still foreclosing at a steady beat every month. As reported by Warren Vieth, a Writer for the Los Angeles Times on 1/3/04, "South Carolina is one of 11 states still classified as being in a recession by Economy.com, a research firm. Industrial production is falling; household balance sheets are unraveling. Bankruptcies and mortgage foreclosures are at all-time highs". In all the research done for this book, Mr. Vieth's premise is substantiated. Your time is valuable, so this information is designed to take you step by step through each chapter without taking up your time with "fluff". Every foreclosed home is a lost opportunity for you.

Chapter Two

"THE PLAYERS"

Short Sales are booming. There is an element of confusion about how the Short Sale works. After all, if you do not understand how it works, you will find it difficult to explain it to your Sellers. The "Players" are the key people you will be negotiating with as you seek approvals on your Short Sale offer. They are typically the Investor, the Mortgage Company or "Servicer", and the Mortgage Insurance, or "MI" Company. They are the most dominate players in the Short Sale game. But, other players, like Second liens, judgment holders, and creditors with liens, can enter the game at any point. The object of the game is to put the puzzle pieces together by determining which player is the *most* important for your offer.

Let's start at the beginning of the game with the original mortgage loan. The money for the original loan actually comes from a large source of Investors like Freddie Mac, Fannie Mae, VA, and FHA. Once the loan is closed, it is assigned to a Servicer (Seller's Mortgage Company). The loan documents are sent to the Servicer, who will monitor payments and escrows (Taxes, Hazard Insurance, and Mortgage Insurance). The Servicer also monitors Collections, Bankruptcy, Foreclosure, and Loss Mitigation.

Loss Mitigators are Specialists at mitigating losses for the Investor, and work for either the Servicer or one of Investor's Outsource Companies.

They are required to review your Short Sale offer under specific Investor guidelines. Loss Mitigators are responsible for negotiating the very best "Alternative to Foreclosure" for the Investor and the delinquent Seller. Most Sellers only correspond with the Servicer since the Servicer collects their payments each month. The do not know anything about the Investor.

To review so far, we have the Investor, who lends the money for the original loan. After the loan closing, the loan is assigned to a Servicer, who monitors loan payments, and escrows. If the loan becomes delinquent, the Servicer must follow Investor guidelines for Collections, Bankruptcy, Foreclosure, and Loss Mitigation.

Another key player is the MI Company. Most Agents and Sellers are not familiar with this company. Here's a little known Secret…the MI Company is probably the *most important* player in the Short Sale approval/ closing process. The Investor will seldom approve the Short Sale without the MI's approval, if needed. You will find more information on the MI Company in Chapter Ten, *"What is the MI Company?"*

The MI Company provides insurance coverage for the Investor, not the Seller. This insurance covers losses due to delinquency and foreclose. So, for instance, if the MI Company insures the loan for 25%, they would cover up to 25% of the "Total Debt" payoff, which includes all fees and costs. FHA loans are insured by HUD (US Department of Housing and Urban Development). Therefore, FHA loans resulting in a Short Sale must be approved under HUD guidelines. Some Servicers staff Loss Mitigators with HUD "delegated authority", which allows them to negotiate and approve Short Sales on HUD's behalf. Conventional loans have a variety of different MI Companies.

Loss Mitigators, sometimes referred to as Negotiators, or Account Representatives, practice due diligence on behalf of the Investor. Remember, the delinquent interest, and escrows increase daily, so time is precious. To practice due diligence, the Servicer reviews delinquent loans for Alternatives to Foreclosure, specific to the loan's Investor in an attempt to "stop the bleeding". Alternatives are based on the Seller's ability to maintain the mortgage payment in the future, and/or bring the loan current The Short Sale is a last resort alternative. The Investor will not incur a loss if they can cure the delinquency and avoid foreclosure with the other options.

More often than not, the Collection Department will tell a Seller in foreclosure, "nothing can be done to help them". Loss Mitigators are NOT Collectors. Loss Mitigators are not trying to collect, they are trying to cure the loan from a possible Investor loss. You will hear it in their voices.

Collectors are sometimes unaware the Loss Mitigation group even exists. Keep in mind, Collectors are there to collect. They are often uninformed on any options other than repayment plans. You, and the Sellers, have to be persistent! Don't give up. Someone, somewhere, cares about the loss. Don't stop until you have spoken with someone in the Loss Mitigation Department. If there is no Loss Mitigation Department, then it's better to find out now, rather than after you have expended your time or money.

Ask to be transferred to Loss Mitigation, Default Management, Foreclosure, or Bankruptcy for assistance. One of those departments probably works directly with Loss Mitigation at most Servicers. No matter if the Servicer owns the loan, or is servicing the loan for a major Investor, I guarantee you, <u>Someone</u> cares.

Ever so often, the Seller will contact a knowledgeable Collector who guides them to the Loss Mitigation group for Short Sale help. These lucky people just saved themselves from further frustration around automated phone systems and uninterested people. Encourage your Sellers to be persistent. It will pay off!

Most delinquent Sellers believe there is no other option, but to foreclosure. Losing their home is imminent, so they panic; either walking away or turning to an attorney for help. They have no idea what is going to happen next. Is the Sheriff, or police, are going to show up at their door with boxes in hand? You may be the Angel, or the knight in shining armor these people have been praying for!

1st Player
Investor: lends the actual funds for the original mortgage loan, and assigns the loan to a Servicer.

2nd Player
Servicer: monitors the loan for the Investor, and acts on their behalf when a loan becomes delinquent.

3rd Player
MI Company: insures the loan by a percentage of the Total Debt payoff, including all fees and costs. They will pay the Investor a percentage (%) of the Total Debt payoff for losses incurred on a Short Sale, or Foreclosure.

4th Player
Loss Mitigator: works for the Servicer on behalf of the Investor. They will analyze the Seller's financial information and submit offers to the Investor, and/or MI Company, for Short Sale approval. The Investor's approval letter for the closing will come directly from the Loss Mitigator.

Chapter Three

A LITTLE HISTORY

Agents, Nationwide, have expressed a desire for Short Sale information and training. Short Sales are really nothing new. But, because there are so many unknown factors, Agents tend to shy away from them. The evolution of the Short Sale process has been simplified over the past 15 years, and is now easier than *ever* before. The Short Sale is the most lucrative "Alternative to Foreclosure" option for the Investors. Other options, like repayment, forbearance, and modification plans are available, but the Seller must financially qualify, and have a cash contribution towards the delinquency.

Economic troubles started brewing in the mid 1980's when unemployment and bankruptcies skyrocketed. The Resolution Trust Corporation, or "RTC", took over delinquent mortgages from the Savings and Loans fiasco. Some of you may remember those days, when Agents lost Buyers, commissions, and faith, when attempting to sell off the RTC Inventory in a saturated market. The process to submit a Short Sale offer on these properties was so difficult, and detailed, it was not cost effective for anyone involved. Buyers, Sellers, and Agents walked away frustrated after wasting their valuable time and money. This left a lasting impression on the Real Estate community for many years to come.

As businesses continued to fail, the economy sank deeper, and unemployment rose. Foreclosures increased sharply, catching the banking industry off guard. They soon found themselves, not only in the banking business, but also in the Real Estate business. The courts became so back logged, homes would literally sit, abandoned for *years,* before finally foreclosing. **True story**: In 1990 my neighbor and I stood in our yards looking at a home across the street that had been abandoned by our, now divorced, neighbor for over two years. Neighbors took turns mowing the yard and protecting it. We figured if the Investor didn't do anything for the next several years, we'd probably have squatter rights!

Foreclosure is the "legal" action of taking the asset (the home) back from a delinquent Seller. Once the home is placed in the Investor's REO inventory, it is marketed in an attempt to recoup all, or part, of the Total Debt payoff. The Investors of yesteryear did not realize how much the length of time *before* and *after* the foreclosure, was costing them in unnecessary losses. Foreclosure legal fees and delinquent interest accumulates daily and is added to the Total Debt payoff. If the property sells at foreclosure for *less* than the Total Debt payoff, the shortage would be considered a loss to the Investor, or MI Company (if covered).

In the 1980's and early 1990's, the Servicer had few Alternatives to Foreclosure. Collection efforts were often brutal and severe, sometimes causing the Sellers to abandon the property, or file bankruptcy. It was pretty much a "pay up, or get out" period in banking history. There was no mercy for the typical Seller who was unemployed with no relief in sight. Some Sellers tried to sell their homes to save themselves from foreclosure, but the loss of value made it impossible to get offers that would satisfy the Investors. Sellers walked away from their homes and debts, causing huge

Investor losses. The Real Estate market became saturated with foreclosed homes, causing home values to plummet, even further.

Incidentally, during the delinquency and foreclosure action, Servicers are responsible for the payment of Real Estate Taxes, Hazard Insurance and monthly Mortgage Insurance premiums, if needed. The Servicer can not let any of these escrow items go unpaid for fear of tax sales, lapse of MI coverage, and lack of insurance coverage to protect the asset. Since no mortgage payments are being made during the delinquency, these extra expenses, along with the daily accrued interest, cause the payoff to rise with each passing day.

To top it all off, in the 1990's foreclosures in some States were taking up to 24 months! And, then, *after* the foreclosure sale, an Investor-Approved Agent is assigned to list the "Real Estate Owned" home until an offer is received. Location, economic climate, and property condition determine the length of time the home sits on the market as an REO. Once net proceeds from an REO closing are applied toward the Total Debt payoff, the total loss to the Investor can be calculated. The Seller will have a judgment placed against them (State permitting) whether they have the ability to pay the judgment, or not.

Originally, this seemed like a good idea; a kind of punishment. The judgment's purpose was to prevent Sellers from purchasing another home, a car, or selling anything of value without paying off the judgment first. Problem with this theory was, financially, the entire Country was in the same position. It wasn't long before foreclosures, bankruptcies, and judgments on credit reports became commonplace, and uneventful. Those were hard times for everyone.

Investors began analyzing "Pre"-Foreclosures, compared to "Post"-Foreclosure losses. Hence, the Pre-Foreclosure Short Sale was born. Investors integrated the Short Sale in with other options designed to help cure delinquent loans.

Investors discovered by working with these Sellers on Short Sales, they could reduce their losses significantly. All Investors use a Short Sale formula consisting of percentages and figures to help compare their losses between the Short Sale and the foreclosure. The formula is more complex and precise, but here is an example: **$200,000 Total Debt payoff – $150,000 appraised or fair market value = $50,000 potential loss. If the Short Sale offer comes in at $160,000 net, the Investor would save $10,000.** The Investor can take a $40,000 loss today with your Short Sale offer, or they can take the $50,000 loss PLUS legal fees, additional delinquent interest, taxes, insurance fees, preservation expenses, maintenance, and so on. The Short Sale evolution continued to gain popularity as other Investors recognized the benefits of Short Sales.

Today almost all Servicers have some type of Loss Mitigation Department specializing in a variety of Investor approved Loss Mitigation options. As it was in the past, the Servicer is still responsible for collection attempts. Investor guidelines assure the Servicer is being pro-active on Short Sales and other options to save the Investor from further losses. Reducing timeframes on foreclosure and marketing, reduces the losses dramatically.

Remember in "The Players", the Servicer only "services" the loan for the Investor. The Servicer seldom incurs losses, as a majority of mortgage loans are covered with MI Insurance. Generally the Servicer only incurs losses on loans *they* own, or loans when the MI Company has dropped their coverage due to reasons relating to their Servicing Agreement. Short Sale approvals for loans owned by the Servicer will be at their discretion. Otherwise, Short Sale approval will be obtained from the Investor or the MI Company, or both, depending on the amount of the loss and insurance coverage.

Now it's time to get started. The following chapters of this book will take you step by step through Short Sales. The knowledge and experience you receive, will prepare you for your first Short Sale closing. You will embark on a new frontier where others dare not tread. Remember, the average Agent will refuse to list a Short Sale. That's when your Short Sale knowledge will pay off!

NOTES

Chapter Four

MY SELLERS DON'T UNDERSTAND!

Some Sellers are going to be a little gun-shy. They may have been trying to sell their homes for a long time, but because they are not aware of the Investor's Short Sale option, they have it listed way too high. Many Sellers complain their Agents set the listing price too high; have the listing for over a year, and then no longer show interest in the home. It really isn't the Agent's fault. They are only doing what they think is right; listing for a full payoff of the mortgage, plus their commission. Because the home is listed unreasonably high, the Agent eventually loses interest, and no longer wants to spend their own money on a losing battle. There is always great joy in hearing an Agent's voice change from one of despair to one of hope when hearing about the Short Sale. So don't worry if you have already had your listing a long time, and are just now finding out about the Short Sale. You still have time to make your money back.

Once you understand the Seller's Short Sale benefits, you will have no problem relaying the information to the Sellers. Sellers hearing about the Short Sale for the first time, feel instant relief. There is great satisfaction in helping people who have come upon hard times. These are not your normal, run-of-the-mill, Sellers. They are going through divorces, unemployment, death, and illness in their lives. They are not moving away to a beautiful new home, or have an exciting new job opportunity in another State. Instead, they are losing every dime they ever invested in the home. Some pray for help; some become bitter, and resentful. Whatever the case, they will appreciate your compassionate help. Your expertise, experience, and knowledge will be exactly what they need to hear. Some skeptical Sellers just won't accept the help. Ask them to contact their attorney for counseling about the program. Offer to outline the benefits of the Short Sale for their attorney, or refer the attorney to the Loss Mitigator. This assures the Seller of the legitimacy of the "too good to be true" Short Sale program.

You will find most attorneys will strongly back the Short Sale and encourage their clients to take the opportunity to find relief from judgments, IRS tax consequences, and credit blemishes. Some attorneys push the bankruptcy since it's easy for the Sellers, and it stops the foreclosure action. But, many Bankruptcy Attorneys say the Short Sale is the better option for their clients. After all, the Bankruptcy Attorney can always have the Seller file after the Short Sale is closed. They will not have to worry about including the property, and settling with the Investor later.

Always have the Seller Sign and date a *Seller's Authorization Form* as seen in Forms at the end of this book. Make this form a part of the Short Sale financial package you present to the Seller at your list agreement meeting. The *Seller's Authorization Form* gives the Servicer, or anyone else connected to the approval process, permission to give out private information about the Seller's mortgage account. In lieu of an *Authorization Form*, the Seller can also handwrite a short letter addressed to "Whom it May Concern". The letter, or *Seller's Authorization* Form, must be signed, and dated by the Sellers before it is acceptable. The typical information you will want from the Servicer will be: **payment due date, foreclosure status, and estimated full payoff**. You can also utilize the *Seller's Questionnaire* to help put the Short Sale puzzle pieces together. When you have the right pieces, you will see the whole picture. This questionnaire provides you with all the information needed by the Loss Mitigator to determine the likelihood of an approved Short Sale.

The Seller will need to complete a financial package and return it to the Servicer's Loss Mitigation Department. Some Sellers find the disclosure of personal financial information too invasive, or difficult to complete. The financial package is very important, so you may have to guide them through the documentation to be sure the package is completed before sending it to the Loss Mitigator. Sellers seem to find it overwhelming when they receive the requirements on paper, but it is relatively simple when you break it down for them. Short Sales are rarely approved on offers when there is no financial package from the Sellers. The only time a Seller would not need to submit a financial package is when they are protected by bankruptcy, or deceased.

The benefits are fairly standard, but they can also be extremely confusing. Although every scenario is different, the First lien (conventional loan) will, typically, release the Seller from the remaining debt (after subtracting the Short Sale net proceeds, from their Total Debt payoff), remove foreclosure credit bureau blemishes, and in most cases, exempt the Sellers from the tax consequences of a 1099 capital gains filing to the IRS. So, let's break it down...

Forgiveness of debt basically relieves the Seller from judgments, or even garnishment of wages, in some states. The judgment would be calculated after all possible funds, and MI claims, have been applied. The judgment is placed on the Seller's credit report for all to see. Judgments are designed to prohibit the Seller from buying or selling anything without satisfying the judgment, first. Of course, some creative people have found ways around the judgment, and seem to be able to continue their lives. But, Sellers who need clear credit for business, career, or personal reasons, feel the forgiveness of debt is a very important benefit. The judgment remains in force for several years, with the right to renew. Collections will most likely continue, as well. As mentioned before, some States even garnish wages! This would mean a portion of the judgment amount would be deducted directly from the Seller's wages, which can be very damaging to Sellers, personally *and* professionally. Their employer and co-workers are now aware of their "dirty laundry".

With a closed Short Sale, a judgment will **not** be placed against the Seller for Fannie Mae, Freddie Mac, VA, or FHA loan. However, there are a few Investors, and other liens, who will not give up their rights to pursue the Sellers after closing. This is more common with Secondary liens who may agree to settle for less than total amount owed, but retain their right to pursue the Seller after closing the Short Sale. These liens may set up payment plans, place judgments, and/or assign the account to a Collection Agency even if they approve the Short payoff. Even so, the Seller will still be in a better bargaining position after the closing, since the remaining debt is now "unsecured". When the title transfers to the Buyers at closing, the debt is no longer attached to the house. If the Seller's financial hardship includes numerous other debts, like credit cards, they may want to seek legal council regarding bankruptcy - *after* the closing.

Another benefit is removal of the FORECLOSURE from the Seller's credit report. While the foreclosure is active, the notice will remain on the credit report until the loan has either foreclosed, or an approved Short Sale is **closed**. The foreclosure is not stopped, or delayed during the listing, or upon receiving an offer. A foreclosure postponement may be requested to allow time to close on an "approved" Short Sale offer. The Loss Mitigator will require an executed contract or offer, Title Company pre-settlement statement or HUD, and the Buyer's loan approval letter (not commitment letter). Most Investors are reasonable on allowing postponements, but may require the Seller to pay any postponement fees, or costs. **NOTE:** The legal fees and filings of the foreclosure continue during the **ENTIRE** Short Sale process. Make sure the Seller understands that the foreclosure action will **not stop**.

Late mortgage payments reported to the Credit Bureau by the Servicer, cannot be removed, or altered, in any way. The Credit Bureau does not allow this as it would jeopardize the integrity of their system. However, once the Short Sale has closed, the foreclosure notice will be removed and replaced with other verbiage, like "paid in full", "settled", or "settled for less than owed".

All of these "other verbiage" options are better for the Seller than a Foreclose notice. Additionally, the Sellers will be able to qualify on rental applications or purchase another home in the future without having to disclose a foreclosure on their Home Loan Application. After all, the home did **NOT** foreclose. This has a large impact on the Seller's future credit worthiness. Some self-employed Sellers who have failed businesses need the ability to start up a new business at a later time with clear credit.

Finally, the exemption from the 1099 consequences. This benefit can be the Most Important of all. Bare in mind, I am not an Attorney or CPA, and have gathered this information through years of experience as a Loss Mitigator for Freddie Mac and Fannie Mae. To explain this simply, when the Investor incurs a loss on the loan; they have a "capital loss". Because the Seller is the *cause* of the loss; the Seller has a "capital gain". Bottom line is, the Seller will be responsible for taxes on the amount the Servicer reports on the 1099 to the IRS. The Seller will receive a 1099 (similar to a W-2) which should be filed with their yearly income tax return. You can imagine the financial consequences if you were taxed on, let's say $25,000-$50,000, extra income you never received! This just doesn't make sense to the Seller. They can not comprehend why they would be taxed on income they never received??? Explain it as I have, and they will see the logic. Logical or not, it can be financially devastating for the Seller.

Whereas, the other two benefits are standard across the board – the 1099 exemption is **NOT**. There are certain Servicers who file the 1099 *regardless* of the Short Sale approval. But, all Fannie Mae and Freddie Mac loans are exempt. Since they are the two largest Investors in the USA, the majority of your Short Sales will fall within this exemption. VA and FHA loans are **not** exempt. The Servicer's Guidelines for VA & HUD (FHA loans) require they file the 1099, so be sure to ask the Loss Mitigator what type of loan you are dealing with, so you can relay the correct benefits to the Seller. When the Servicer monitors a loan for another Mortgage Company, the owner of the loan is called a "Private Investor". The Private Investor has the option to file, or not file, the 1099. Try to make this part of your final negotiations, but realize they have the final word. If you, or your Seller, still have questions about the 1099, consult a Tax Attorney, or CPA. They will be able to calculate the taxes due on the 1099 amount. This will give you an idea of the Seller's benefits/consequences. Sometimes, even if there *are* tax consequences, the Seller will still be better off with a Short Sale.

At the Short Sale closing, the Seller is **prohibited from accepting any money** at all on conventional loans, like Fannie Mae and Freddie Mac. But, on FHA loans, Sellers are offered an "incentive" for their cooperation during the marketing, and closing, of the Short Sale. These "FHA Approved" Sellers will receive $750 at closing for their participation, and an additional $250, if the home closes within 3 months! The Investors want the home to close as quickly as possible. What an advantage for YOU!

All Short Sales, whether conventional or government, have pretty standard benefits. All Investors use a similar financial statement and require the same financial information from the Seller. They continue to make changes in their systems to promote streamlining. With the exception of the above "incentive" and the 1099 filing, there are no other major differences between the government and conventional loan guidelines.

For a more in-depth review of the Seller's benefits, please see Chapter Eighteen, *"Seller's Short Sale Benefits - Review"*. This review will give you additional tips and suggestions on the above Seller benefits. Also see the *Foreclosure Time Table* for foreclosure times, redemption periods, and deficiency rights.

NOTES

Chapter Five

GETTING STARTED

Fortunately, for Short Sale Agents, the abundance of available Short Sales are based on the economic climate of the Country. There never seems to be a shortage of hardships like unemployment, illness, injury, divorce, or death. Short Sales have continued to increase steadily in the last decade, which serves as an economic indicator in our Country. In almost all cases, Short Sale approval is contingent upon the Seller's hardship reasons, like those listed above. I say "almost" because there are just a few exceptions to the rule. As an example: If the Seller has no hardship, but is willing to sign a note with the MI Company/Investor for the remaining balance of the payoff, they can still receive the benefits. You will have to be creative sometimes to find solutions. It's part of the game! Refer to the listing of "Financial Hardships" in *Forms*.

Although Investors offer other options, or "Alternatives to Foreclosure", such as repayment plans, forbearance plans, and modifications, the Short Sale option produces a much higher savings for the Investor over any other option they offer. Most of these "other" options will be offered to your Seller first. If the Seller qualifies for one of the above options and has an interest in keeping the home, the Short Sale will be a secondary option. There are times when Sellers either do not qualify, or fail to perform on the other plans. Then, they may be knocking on your door again!

When a Seller has an acceptable hardship, does not want to keep the home, **and** has negative equity, it is considered a "Short Sale". Basically, the net sales proceeds from the closing will be "short of a full payoff". A full payoff usually includes all legal fees, delinquent interest, late charges, NSF fees, and so on. Sellers mistakenly think the payoff is the "Unpaid Principal Balance", or UPB, of the loan. They are not accounting for the months of delinquent interest, and fees. Remember, while mortgage payments are not being made, the interest continues to click away, daily.

To determine how knowledgeable your Seller is on their mortgage payoff, ask the Seller two questions. Instead of just asking "what is the balance", also ask "what is the full payoff"? If you get the same answers, or a blank stare, then you will want the Seller to order a payoff so there will be no surprises once you get an offer. Just knowing this little trick could save you from making this common mistake. As you will see in Chapter Thirteen, *"The Short Sale Offer"*, falling short of funds needed to close after the offer has been executed, can lead to legal ramifications for you, and the Sellers.

There are a few tricks of the trade, which will make the Short Sale the easiest, and most gratifying, sale you will ever close. The sooner you get started; the quicker you will be sitting at the closing table. Someone once said, "the hardest part of success is GETTING STARTED."

Once you have the *Seller's Questionnaire* completed, and all the figures in front of you, it will be easier to estimate whether the sale will be short, or not. Once you have determined the net proceeds will be short, contact the Loss Mitigation Department for **all** liens involved in the shortage.

There are a variety of ways to search for Short Sales. Some typical sources are **foreclosure, bankruptcy, divorce** filings, and the **obituaries**. Foreclosures and bankruptcies are public knowledge, and can be found in the paper, at your local County Courthouse, or on the Web. Typically FSBO's and obituaries are found in the local papers, but may require an occasional drive-by in areas suffering from loss of value. It's just that easy! You don't have to be a brain surgeon, just have to be organized, and work hard.

Use the **FORECLOSURE TIME TABLE** on the next page to determine the amount of time remaining before foreclosure. You must sell the home within this "estimate" State timeframe. Note Redemption and deficiency rights in your State, also. These factors will have a bearing on the Investor's willingness to approve the Short Sale. Since redemptions cause delays in foreclosure, and the lack of deficiency rights make pursuing a judgment almost impossible, the Investor will be interested in your offers in those States. If a foreclosure sale date has already been set, you may request a foreclosure postponement through the Loss Mitigator. But, only on offers with a "pending" closing date.

Loss Mitigation Departments work directly with their Foreclosure Department, and the Foreclosure Attorney, in coordinating the foreclosure postponement process. FYI - **Foreclosures** in GA and TX have what is called *"Super Tuesday"* foreclosure sale dates. These two States have only one foreclosure auction per month; held on the first Tuesday of each month. Both are considered "restart states", meaning the foreclosure sale cannot be postponed, or put on "hold". The entire foreclosure must be canceled to allow for delays in your closing. If the Short Sale closing should happen to fall out, the foreclosure action would have to be restarted

FORECLOSURE TIME TABLE

STATE	# of Mos	Redemption	Deficiency
AK / Alaska	4	None	YES
AL / Alabama	3	12 months	YES
AR / Arkansas	3	None	YES
AZ / Arizona	4	None	YES
CA / California	4	None	NO
CO / Colorado	5	75 Days	YES
CT / Connecticut	6	None	YES
CT / Connecticut	6	None	YES
DC / District of Columbia	4	None	YES
DE / Delaware	7	None	YES
FL / Florida	5	10 days	COT
GA / Georgia	2	None	YES
HI / Hawaii	4	None	YES
IA / Iowa	6	0 - 12 months	YES
ID / Idaho	6	None	YES
IL / Illinois	10	12 days	YES
IN / Indiana	7	None	YES
KS / Kansas	4	3 -12 months	YES
KY / Kentucky	5	45 to 60 days	YES
LA / Louisiana	6	None	YES
MA / Massachusetts	4	None	YES
MD / Maryland	2	45 to 60 days	YES
ME / Maine	10	None	YES
MI / Michigan	2	6 - 12 months	YES
MN / Minnesota	3	6 - 12 months	NO
MO / Missouri	2	None	YES
MS / Mississippi	3	None	NO
MT / Montana	5	None	NO
NC / North Carolina	4	10 days	YES
ND / North Dakota	5	2-12 months	NO
NE / Nebraska	4	None	YES
NH / New Hampshire	3	None	YES
NJ / New Jersey	10	10 days	YES
NM / New Mexico	6	None	YES
NV / Nevada	4	None	YES
NY / New York	8	None	YES
OH / Ohio	7	45 to 60 days	YES
OK / Oklahoma	7	15 days	YES
OR / Oregon	5	None	YES
PA / Pennsylvania	9	None	YES
RI / Rhode Island	3	None	YES
SC / South Carolina	6	30 days	YES
SD / South Dakota	5	6-12 months	YES
TN / Tennessee	2	None	YES
TX / Texas	2	None	YES
UT / Utah	5	None	YES
VA / Virginia	2	None	YES
VT / Vermont	10	None	YES
WA / Washington	5	None	YES
WI / Wisconsin	10	None	YES
WV / West Virginia	2	None	NO
WY / Wyoming	3	3 - 4 months	YES

costing the Investor twice the legal fees. Foreclosure postponement costs vary in every State, and range from $0.00 to $2,000. The Seller can sometimes be held responsible for these extra fees. This is especially true if the Seller waited until the last minute to get their financial package, and/or offer, to the Loss Mitigator for review.

CO, IA, ND, and SC do not have costs to postpone a foreclosure sale. But, CT, DC, DE, HI, MA, MD, NH, NM, OH, and RI have postponement costs of $500, and above. You can gauge your negotiation of the postponement, based on the cost in your State. Of course, the cheaper it is to postpone, the greater the chances of getting it approved.

Be sure you give the Loss Mitigator enough time to process the postponement request. About 2-3 weeks prior to the foreclosure sale date is usually ample time for the Loss Mitigator to receive all approvals needed to secure the postponement. Since the clock is ticking, you will need to monitor the listing much closer, and be in constant contact with the Loss Mitigator. Once the postponement has been approved, ask the Seller to call the Foreclosure Attorney and verify the "hold" status of the foreclosure. THIS IS VERY IMPORTANT. You stand to lose the Short Sale COMPLETELY at this point, so be conscientious.

Bankruptcy filings can also be a good source for Short Sales. If the Seller filed a Chapter 7 bankruptcy, the Investor and/or other liens may be more willing to consider a Short Sale, and avoid the delays caused by the bankruptcy. The only exception here are VA loans. VA will not approve a any loan workout on a discharged Chapter 7, unless the Seller has "reaffirmed" their debt through the bankruptcy. As explained in further detail in Chapter Eleven, "*My Seller Has Filed Bankruptcy*", the Seller participating in a Chapter 13 bankruptcy is not a likely candidate for a Short Sale. This type of bankruptcy indicates the Sellers may be on a court appointed payment plan. Because a Trustee is assigned to this plan, their approval would be needed for a Short Sale.

Divorces often necessitate selling the marital residence. Since marital problems are commonly a result of financial problems (and often used as a weapon in quarrels) the home can fall behind quickly. If the Sellers are divorced, it is possible one of them signed a quit claim deed (QCD) when the divorce was finalized.

Since the Seller who signed the QCD no longer lives in the home, they think they have no further financial obligation. But, when the Seller who occupies the home stops making payments, and the home heads toward foreclosure, they discover "both" Sellers are held responsible. Once the Collection calls and letters start, the weapon has been loaded. What they don't understand is that although the QCD removes one of the Sellers from the Title, the debtors on the *loan* do not change. Both Sellers will be held liable for deficiency judgments (where permitted), 1099 tax consequences, and a foreclosure notice on both credit reports once the property forecloses. In the Short Sale, both Sellers share equal responsibility, which can be negotiated between the Sellers, and their Divorce Attorneys.

Try not to counsel the Sellers on marital matters. Make it clear from the beginning that your purpose is to relieve them from this obligation and the consequences of a foreclosure. After they have vented their frustrations, tell them you understand their situation, but they have this one chance of putting this mess behind them, and moving forward without the extra "baggage" created by a foreclosure. They can now settle down, and think logically. Promote teamwork.

If you have the attention of one Seller, but the other one is refusing to participate, get the name and number of his/her Divorce Attorney. Whereas the bruised heart of the non-participator can only see revenge, the Divorce Attorney will be very interested in how the Short Sale can resolve their client's future financial problems.

If no QCD was signed through the divorce, both Sellers will need to participate in the signing of all documents from the listing to the closing. Separate financial packages are required for *both* Sellers, *if* they are both listed on the mortgage loan. Do not combine income and expenses for Sellers who live separately, because if a note is required by the Investor or MI Company, they will base the amount, and monthly payments, on each Seller's individual ability to pay.

FSBO ("For Sale by Owner") also indicate there may be financial troubles brewing. Many of the current FSBO's on the market are mortgage loans in default, or foreclosure. The Sellers probably have already done the math, and have determined they cannot pay a commission. The Investor of a loan in foreclosure encourages you to submit offers and will **guarantee** your commission. These are often homes other Agents have refused to list. Short Sales allow you to list those homes for fair market value and close immediately! For the first time, be able to offer the FSBO Seller something no other Agent has been able to before. Tap into a whole new market. Get those listings you have never been able to obtain previously. Just imagine having an opportunity to increase your listings with FSBO's in your area.

And, finally, as morbid as it may sound; homes of the **Deceased Seller**. It's kind of an ambulance chasing thing, but there is a need for the family to liquidate all of their loved ones assets. Of course, be respectful and do not call too soon! The family will not want to talk about it until they begin to settle the deceased's debts. You will want to wait for at least a month or two, with an occasional drive by to see if it is occupied by family members, or abandoned. If the address is posted as a foreclosure, then it is time to make contact. If family members plan to assume the responsibility of the home, you can be helpful and suggest contacting the Servicer's Loss Mitigation Department.

An option commonly known as an "assumption" can be performed by modifying the loan and adding the new owners (family members) to the loan, and Title. They will be required to complete a financial package and all required financial documentation. This option gives a "financially qualified" relative the opportunity to assume the mortgage with it's current unpaid principal balance, or UPB. The delinquent amount can be added to the UPB with the term of the loan extended out for up to 40 yrs. If the assumption option is not feasible, the family members may remember your help, and call you for the listing.

All foreclosures have a story behind them. Some Sellers need to sell before they lose their home to foreclosure. The time is ticking. Of course, if there is enough equity to pay the loan off in full, there is no problem. The listing and the closing would be standard to the industry.

Timing is everything! Once the loan is delinquent for 60 days or more, and Collection efforts have failed, the Servicer can start the foreclosure legal action by sending a "Breach Letter". This letter will give a foreclosure referral date, which is 30 days after the date of the letter. After this date expires, the Servicer can refer the delinquent mortgage account to a Foreclosure Attorney, "kaa-ching", the legal fees have now begun. The letter also specifies a total amount due and the total UPB of the loan. It is during this 30 day breach period, the Seller can cure the loan in full by reinstating, selling, or refinancing.

The Breach Letter contains very important information on the loan, including a payoff good through a specific date. It's usually sent by *certified* mail from the Servicer, or the Foreclosure Attorney. The Sellers have now been legally notified of the pending foreclosure action against them, whether they accept the certified mail, or not. Encourage them to accept this letter, since the information contained within will help the Sellers make important decisions on what to do next.

It's during this 30 day breach period that you chance to lose your Sellers completely. Some just walk away, abandoning the home. Or file bankruptcy, causing a long delay for pending offers. When the Sellers contact the Loss Mitigator, they will be given a chance to cure the loan and remain in the property by choosing one of the other "Alternative to Foreclosure" options. If the Seller is prepared to receive this breach letter, they will not panic and do something they, and you, will regret later.

Once the loan has been referred to foreclosure, the Seller begins receiving all kinds of mail from Credit Counseling Services, Bankruptcy Attorneys, Agents, and Private Investors. It will be difficult for your Seller to decipher between what to keep, and what to trash. They need to pay attention specifically to any correspondence received from their Servicer, or Foreclosure Attorney. If the Seller hasn't already contacted the

Servicer's Loss Mitigation Department, the information they receive from the Mortgage Company correspondence could be the contact information you need to get started on the Short Sale.

Once your Seller has made contact with the Loss Mitigation Department they will receive the Investor's financial package requirements, which consists of a completed financial statement, hardship letter, pay stubs verifying income, bank statements, and tax returns or W-2 statements for the past two years.

Now it's time to get started!

Chapter Six

__LISTING A SHORT SALE__

The listing of the Short Sale is a good time to decide whether to move forward, or pull back. So far you have only expended time, and even though time is money, you have had no out-of-pocket expenses, yet. By now, you should have a *Seller's Authorization Form* completed and signed, and the information from the *Seller's Questionnaire*. The Sellers should have the financial package, and all requested financial documentation completed, before anyone signs the listing. Now is the time to put the puzzle pieces together. See the whole picture. This is the game of "Success". Successful negotiating skills and human insight can be applied to any business transaction.

Determine, in your best judgment, how short the net proceeds will be at closing. As you become more experienced, you can fine tune your routine down to a science. Soon, you will be able to quickly review the Seller's financial statement, and payoffs, to see the outline of the puzzle. Utilize the *Seller's Questionnaire* to obtain the number of players, with balances and foreclosure status. Determine if it's time to sign a listing, or run away. By working smart, and making as few moves as possible, you will turn every Short Sale into personal profit.

Again, the number one mistake Agents make when listing a Short Sale property....when asked for a payoff figure, the Seller usually responds with the "Unpaid Principal Balance". The payoff and the UPB are two different amounts, and can vary greatly. The Agent typically adds together the first lien unpaid principle balance with any other liens, and tops it off with their commission and anticipated closing costs. This is quite common, and creates an extremely long, and unprofitable listing on Short Sales. Short Sale knowledge and proven techniques will help you avoid those mistakes that *cost* you time, and money.

It's really very simple. Determine the fair market value, instead of the payoff, and then increase the list price for marketing purposes. Now you can see why Short Sales sell so fast! They are priced right for the market. No need to figure in your commission; it's guaranteed by the Investor once they approve your Short Sale offer.

But, before signing the listing agreement, call the Servicer's Loss Mitigation Department, and find out what they will need to open a file. They will want a fax of your listing agreement and the financial package, completed by the Seller. It's best to hold off on signing the listing until *after* talking to the Loss Mitigator as they may want to participate in setting the list price. The Loss Mitigator will ultimately have control of the increases, reductions, and countering from this point on. Of course, every Loss Mitigator is different, and may be under different Investor guidelines. They may ask your opinion on the value, and request you be available to give access to their Agent, or Appraiser, who will be contracted to obtain a value on behalf of the Investor of the loan. The listing price will be determined by the property's fair market, or appraised value. See Chapter Seven, *"Fair Market Value"*, for more details.

The listing procedure is really pretty standard – just use your State approved listing agreement. There are just a few pointers to keep in mind. *Always* make a Short Sale listing "Subject to Investor Approval" and sold in an "as-is" condition. You will see these clauses come up again when you start receiving offers.

Once the listing is signed, and placed in your local MLS, you will specify the same clauses in the MLS, too. More, and more Agents are now specializing in Short Sales, so hopefully when an offer is received, the Buyer's Agent will also be knowledgeable about the process. When both Agents are experienced in Short Sales, the closing is a smoother transaction.

Now, with the listing "Subject to Investor Approval", the responsibility for negotiating any future reductions and offers will lie with the Loss Mitigator at the Seller's Servicer. Once you have made contact with the Loss Mitigator, and have faxed the previously mentioned Seller's information and a copy of the listing agreement, they will be in charge. They may call you once, or twice a month to check on the showing activity and request reductions until you hit the target price range for offers to start rolling in. Stay in contact whether they call you, or you call them. The Loss Mitigator will now replace the Sellers when reducing list prices, accepting or countering offers, and obtaining Investor approval on all offers. The Seller's participation, once qualified financially, will only be signing the initial listing and reductions, signing the offer once it is "Subject to Investor approval", and signing the deed transfer at closing.

Most Loss Mitigators are willing to listen to your opinions since you know the area much better than they. But, in most cases, you will have to follow the Loss Mitigator's instructions. The Loss Mitigator will also have a good estimate of time on the foreclosure process in your State. As the foreclosure nears, you can get more aggressive with your listing price reductions. You have to beat the foreclosure time clock, or you will be eliminated from the game. The following are suggestions on your listings that will help you work smart.

First, keep the listing term short. 3 - 6 months is probably sufficient, since Short Sales typically close within the first 6 months. If your Broker requires one year listing agreements, that is fine. The Seller may be able to tell you if the foreclosure sale date has been set by legal notices, or correspondence, received from the Servicer's Foreclosure Attorney.

The Seller will probably need to make the initial attorney contact, and fax the *Seller's Authorization Form* to them, before they will speak to outside parties. Once you know the foreclosure status of the property, you will be able to gauge how long you have to market the home. If you do not get an offer before the day of the foreclosure auction, your listing ends at the time of the foreclosure sale. Your listing is valid up until the day of foreclosure, but if you do not have an offer by then, well, let's just say "the fat lady *will* sing". See more on offers in Chapter Thirteen, *"The Short Sale Offer"*.

Second, if you can contact the Loss Mitigation Department <u>before</u> you sign the listing, you will get a feel on whether they have a program in place to obtain approvals on Short Sales, or not. These days, most major Servicers have Loss Mitigation Departments. Ask the Seller for the most recent mortgage statements on all liens. These statements contain contact numbers, account numbers, due dates, and approximate Unpaid Principal

Balances. You can also go online to the Servicer's website and see if they have access numbers under "delinquent" loans. If the Seller calls the Loss Mitigator first, they will send out a list of the required financial documentation and financial statement directly to the Sellers to complete, and return. Once the financial package is completed by the Seller, review it with them to check for completeness. Put yourself in the position of the Investor, and ask the questions they will most likely ask. This way you will have all the answers when you talk with the Loss Mitigator.

Once the financial package has been faxed to the Servicer, it will be reviewed for completeness by a "front end" person before being assigned to a Loss Mitigator. Offers cannot be fully reviewed without a completed financial package. If the Seller is unable to get some of the required documents, they can explain *why* in their "hardship letter". The hardship letter should explain why they are no longer able to make their mortgage payments, and express their desire to sell the home. The hardship reason should directly relate to the due date. If it doesn't, ask the Seller why they became delinquent before, or after, the hardship occurred. The quicker you get a file open with the Loss Mitigator, the quicker you will have the ability to set your listing price.

Some Loss Mitigators, mainly on Second or other liens, do not want the Seller's financial package until an offer is received. Ask the Loss Mitigator to send a financial package to the Seller, anyway. They will want it all at once, when an offer comes in. So, if the Sellers are dragging their feet on the financial package, get them motivated. Keep in mind that all the Loss Mitigation options offered by the Investors are dependent upon the Seller's cooperation, and participation. If you do not have the Seller's cooperation at this point, then you may be wasting your time.

Loss Mitigators will need time to order a market analysis from an Investor approved list of Agents, or Appraisers. If, by chance, you or someone else in your office is called for this Investor value, you will have to decline the request in order to avoid a conflict of interest. I'm sure you can understand the Investor's reasoning. The Loss Mitigator will determine where to set the list price based on valuations like BPO's, CMA's, and Appraisals. With the listing price set at fair market value, the chances of getting an offer are excellent! This can reduce your marketing time significantly.

Once the listing price is agreed upon by the Loss Mitigator, and signed by the Sellers, you will start to receive numerous offers! The Short Sale begins to get exciting now! While other Agents are listing homes at the full payoff, *plus* commission, and sitting on them for a year; you can be listing, advertising, showing, *and* closing within the first three to six months of **your** listing. The quicker the property sells; the less money you spend on MLS fees, advertising, gas, and maintenance issues. The total days on the market is minimized when you are listed at the right price from the very beginning.

Of course, there are always uncontrollable economic factors, like "saturated" market conditions, which can increase the listing period. So, if after a month of marketing, you do not have a steady flow of activity, you should re-evaluate your list price. Simply call the Loss Mitigator and request a reduction. If the list price is already *at* fair market, or appraised value, but still needs to be reduced further; explain the reasons why, and supply new comps to support your argument. The Loss Mitigator is *usually* reasonable, but you will need to show justification for a listing reduction that is lower than the Investor's Agent value.

If the reason for a listing reduction below value is due to specific damages or conditions (i.e. flood, mold, mildew, or other Agent "showing" objections), you may want to present comps, and/or 2-3 repair bids on conditions like the above that can cause the value to fall *below* fair market. These bids will be used, in most cases, only as benchmarks when considering a low offer. Keep the bids handy as they may be needed once an offer is received. Investors would rather sell homes with these types of conditions "prior" to foreclosure to avoid adding a damaged property to their REO inventory. They may even consider a discount on the sales price, if these conditions apply.

Another Short Sale issue is **Manufactured Housing and Mobile Homes**. The Investor usually does not want to take these types of homes back at foreclosure, and into their REO inventory. They find it advantageous to approve Short Sales, instead. The Investor would rather approve a Short Sale on these homes because they have difficulty in procuring a foreclosure, and another reason is the location of most manufactured or mobile homes. They are often in rural, or undesirable areas. Typically, these homes tend to lose value at a much faster pace than a conventionally built home, and they deteriorate even faster once vacated. Loans on mobile or manufactured homes are harder for the Investor to foreclose upon, making them more pliable for negotiation on offers you present. Make the Loss Mitigator aware your listing is a manufactured or mobile home.

Be reasonable when setting the commission rate on the listing. The Investor will probably negotiate a reduced commission percentage once an offer is received. No matter what percentage you set on your listing, the Investor usually negotiates the commission down by at least 1% when offers are reviewed. OK, I'll just say it – the Investor usually wants to lower the commission to 5%. This helps them minimize their losses significantly. But, don't let this discourage you! You can make up the difference by selling the home faster than your other listings.

Now that the home is listed at fair market value, you can reduce the marketing period down to 3-6 months. Additionally, you have increased your listings now. Ultimately, the more listings you have, the more offers you will receive. If you face a reduced commission, ask the Buyer's Agent to split the difference equally. Usually, Agents have out-of-pocket expenses and would rather get something, instead of nothing. Knowing this upfront will keep you from using your energy on anger.

Since you MUST have the Investor's approval, they are not legally bound by your listing agreement with the Seller. The Loss Mitigator is always acting on behalf of the Investor to reduce the total loss and increase the total savings over REO. They will "shave" costs wherever possible. The Loss Mitigator can negotiate *all* points of the offer to help mitigate the losses. They do not have to consult with the Seller on these negotiations.

Of course, the Seller's participation is needed, as they must sign all list reductions and offers, but without the Investor's approval letter, you cannot close a Short Sale. Please keep in mind, the Loss Mitigator may be following specific Investor guidelines when negotiating the closing costs and commission. If you prepare yourself for the reduced commission ahead of time, the shock factor will be minimal. This will enable you to keep your cool, and negotiate to the best of your ability.

In the next chapter, learn how to get the best listing price possible by working with the Investor's Agent on their evaluation of the property.

Chapter Seven

FAIR MARKET VALUE

The Fair Market Value of the property is the target. Once you know where to aim, the Bulls Eye doesn't seem to be quite as difficult to hit. It will be to your advantage to get in on the Short Sale from the beginning, and narrow in on the target. But, if you have already had a listing for some time, and are just discovering the Short Sale, do not despair. You may have time to turn it around, and still profit.

The value of the property sets the "target" sales price. Your goals have changed from trying to make the most cash for the Sellers at closing, to saving the Investor from as much loss as possible. As stated earlier, the Seller's hardship and financial package will verify to the Investor that pursuing a judgment would be wasted time, and money. Once the Sellers let go of any hope for cash at closing, they will be more accepting on price reductions, and countering of offers. By now, the Sellers should understand the main benefit of selling is no longer cash for them, but instead, relief from judgments, 1099 taxes, and damaged credit.

It may take some Sellers time to come to this realization. They are just <u>positive</u> they have built up equity! Show the Seller the comps for other homes in their area, and encourage them to drive-by, and see for themselves. Although this may soften them up a little; they may still be persistent. If that's the case, go ahead and humor them. Agree to set the listing at the price they desire with an agreement to reduce every 2 weeks until showings increase. Ask the Seller to inform you of any pending foreclosure action, and agree to complete the financial package once the listing price drops to within **7% of a total payoff**. **Example: If you had a Payoff = $200,000; List Price = $205,000.   LP $205,000 - $14,350 (7% Total Seller's Closing Costs - 5% Commission; 2% Closing Costs) = $190,650 net proceeds.** The net proceeds would be "short" by $5,000. Use this equation every time you reduce the list price. Just a tip to help you monitor the transition from a "Full Payoff" to a "Short Sale".

Across the Nation, fair market evaluations prepared by Real Estate Agents are called by different names like a BPO (Broker's Price Opinion) or CMA (Comparative Market Analysis). They are basically the same thing - comparing the subject property to other sold properties of comparable style, size, room count, and location. Due to this, we will refer to it as a "value" throughout.

Almost all Investors will order their own value when either an offer, or a financial package is received from the Seller. Their values are usually ordered from an Investor-Approved Agent list. Fannie Mae is the only Investor who requires a full appraisal for Short Sales. Although a "fair market" value is actually more realistic than an appraisal, Fannie Mae often accounts for the difference when negotiating their Short Sales. The Investor knows you can only sell a property for whatever people are willing to pay for it.

Do your homework, first. When preparing your value for a Short Sale, it is *critical* to note any repairs or damage, which could affect the marketability and /or value of the property. While performing your interior inspection, be sure to ask the Seller questions regarding any major repairs such as water damage, roof damage, foundations, fuel tanks, or mold/mildew. These issues can have a monetary impact on the home's marketability, and could be overlooked during the Investor's Agent inspection. Collect any inspection reports and estimates from the Seller on areas of concern. Keep this documentation in your listing file for upcoming offers.

Now that you have a good idea of the interior and exterior condition of your listing, pull comparables, or "comps" from your local Multiple Listing Service (MLS). You probably already pull comps on all your potential listings to advise Sellers of the property's worth, anyway. But, with a Short Sale, the comps you pull may be your saving grace, so keep copies in your listing file.

If no comps are available in the area, or they are too old, pull the closest and newest comps possible. Chances are, the Investor's Agent will run into the same issues. Be sure to make appropriate adjustments on comps for distance from the Subject property. Short Sale battles have been won over the distance of comps from the Subject, alone. This usually only affects rural properties, though.

Most Loss Mitigators will be familiar with the different types of evaluation forms used by Agents, so supply the Loss Mitigator with your value on whatever form you are used to using. Although, Loss Mitigators do not usually <u>require</u> your value, you should send one, regardless. After you have submitted your estimate of fair market value, the Loss Mitigator can now start to help you achieve your target list price.

Make your value as accurate as possible, using the best comps and keeping repair estimates and adjustments reasonable. Remember, your value will be compared to the Investor's Agent value when offers are reviewed for approval. So be extra thorough and complete by including details regarding repairs and other issues on *your* value form. Most forms have a space for Environmental Issue and Repairs. If there is a large discrepancy between the two values, the Investor (or MI Company) will often order another value as a tie breaker. The delay caused by the tie breaker value has lost many a Buyer.

When you submit an accurate value, the Short Sale becomes easier for all involved. You can actually *save* time by doing it right; the first time. Save yourself time, and trouble. If an offer comes in lower than expected, you will be glad you took the extra time to collect information to support the offer. Of course, if the value decreases due to damage occurring during your listing period, take pictures of the damage, and fax repair bids to the Loss Mitigator. If the damage is covered by the Seller's Homeowner Insurance, have the Seller request a visit by an Insurance Adjustor and file a claim. See more about repair contingencies in Chapter Thirteen, *"The Short Sale Offer"*.

Another issue you should mention on your value is Manufactured homes, or Mobile homes. These properties are a concern for the Investor, which makes them more willing to negotiate on the sales price. The State requirements for selling these homes vary, but in most States you will need a Certificate of Attachment. This certificate can be obtained from the County Records, pulled by the DMV, or found in the original Title Policy. Depending upon the year, State, or County, the search for this document could be futile. For this particular reason, the Investor could find it difficult to take clear Title at foreclosure. Even if the Seller wants to keep the property, and qualifies for a modification of the loan, the status of the attachment could prevent the Investor from approving that option. A loan modification must have clear title, which cannot be achieved without delays in the foreclosure time table. The only other options available to the financially "qualified" Seller are repayment and forbearance plans. If the Seller does not have sufficient funds for those options, the Short Sale may be the only option left.

This is why it is very important to perform a thorough inspection of the home. These are all "hot points" that will help in your negotiations and counters with the Investor.

When the Loss Mitigator requests their interior value on behalf of the Investor, they will require a name and number for someone who can give them access to the property. The Investor's value is required in almost every Short Sale, as they will be calculating their savings, risk, and loss based on this value. Another value may also be required by any Second liens who are considering a Short Sale option. These values are very important to your Success in Short Sales. Don't leave this responsibility up to the Seller, unless you feel they are capable of handling it. After all, the value derived from this visit will be your target price during your *entire* listing.

The appraiser, or Investor's Agent, is not familiar with the home and may miss pertinent issues, which could have an impact on the value. Characteristics like a city dump within smelling distance, or a strip club creating traffic issues, needs to be mentioned to the Investor's Agent while they are at the home. If the Investor's Agent is not familiar with surrounding factors, they may miss making adjustments for marketability, or estimate days on the market. Other factors like electrical high wires (unfounded fears), railroad tracks (noise), airports (noise/fumes), or high crime areas (security), should be pointed out.

It is extremely tough to get the value changed after it has been submitted to the Loss Mitigator. The Investor's Agent or Appraiser will defend their value to the end. Since the Loss Mitigator sets the listing price based on the two values, it is in your best interest to spend your time on this part of the Short Sale. The Loss Mitigator will be the one you have to convince when requesting a list reduction, or submitting a low offer.

The Agent providing the Investor's value, should not be the Agent soliciting the listing. The Investor considers this a conflict of interest once offers are received. If you are the Investor's Agent, and unable to list the property, refer the listing to another Broker without conflict. If you also bring in the Buyer, the Investor may also consider this a conflict of interest, too. This conflict can be resolved with a third, unbiased, value.

In cases of value conflict, the MI Company will most likely order another value, as they want to substantiate the loss expected to be paid as a claim to the Investor. If your dispute on the value is valid, it will usually show up in the MI's value. If it doesn't, then you have to move on. List the home price as suggested by the Loss Mitigator; you may be surprised to find out they were right on the target! If you get a higher offer, I'm sure you won't mind when you collect your commission at closing.

The Loss Mitigator may monitor your listing and refer back to fair market value throughout. Although they may set the listing price higher than you like, they can approve a reduced list price after 30 days of marketing with no activity. If the listing price is set too high to generate showings, the Loss Mitigator might suggest ways to increase activity. The Investors are just as anxious to get an offer as you are. Fax your most current comps substantiating any listing reduction requests. Without an offer, the home remains on the market, not benefiting anyone. Remember, the Investor wants to reduce "days on the market" because mortgage interest continues clicking away, daily.

The *value* is the common denominator between an REO and a Short Sale. The value of the asset - is, what it is. So, whether the Investor forecloses, or approves your Short Sale offer, it will not have any affect on the actual value of the home. But the **difference between selling the home today with your offer, or selling the home later as an REO**, will be the clincher for the Investor. This tip can work for you, too. Just knowing this fact will give you the heads up over other Agents who are stumbling through their Short Sales.

To think like the Loss Mitigator, you will need to understand how they figure their savings. The difference in net proceeds from the Short Sale to the REO, is commonly referred to as the Investor's "Savings Over REO". To figure the Savings over REO, the Investor will compare your offer (and net proceeds) against the estimated net proceeds from an REO. *Prove* your offer is better than other offers the Investor will get, if they choose to foreclose. Agents who use this theory are very successful in getting their Short Sales approved. The Investor will approve, or deny, your Short Sale offer based upon which offer produces the most savings. If there is no advantage for the Investor to approve the Short Sale, they will, in some cases, proceed with the foreclosure.

After the Investor calculates their "Savings Over REO", the difference on their loss will be revealed as a negative, or a positive. If the Savings over REO is a negative amount, then the Investor is better off going through with the foreclosure because it indicates there is either enough equity to pay them in full, or not enough of a savings for them with the Short Sale. If it comes out a positive number, they will approve your Short Sale offer.

The formula uses increased costs for an REO, which includes costs occurring *after* the foreclosure. Some of these costs are extended legal fees, delinquent interest, and REO closing costs. Also included are Real Estate commissions, and repairs/maintenance for preservation purposes. Since those factors are what can make, or break, your Short Sale, it is in your best interest to make a list of those items or conditions of the property that could cause a delay in selling as an REO. After all, if the Investor can see delays in selling the home as an REO, they will be more anxious to sell the home now.

So, work smart from the *beginning*. Start with the listing of the Short Sale by setting the price at fair market value. Preparing the ground work first will assure a smoother listing, offer, and closing. Keep your file complete with good comps, notations of damage, environmental conditions, inspection reports, estimates on repairs, and the Seller's financial package. Once you set the list price appropriately, you are well on your way to Success in Short Sales.

Chapter Eight

ENVIRONMENTAL ISSUES

This Chapter will cover Environmental Issues and the best negotiation techniques to use when dealing with the Investor. Environmental conditions can lower the value of the home, and make marketing long and expensive. Some Agents will refuse to list a home with such conditions. And, the Investor does not want to foreclose on the home, as they ultimately end up having to correct the problem, or sell the home cheaply to avoid the costs to repair as an REO. As a Short Sale, they will consider a reduced listing price and/or sales price.

The condition can sometimes be corrected by the Seller, with the help of the Homeowner's Insurance Company. But in most of the following situations, the costs to repair the damages, or environmental conditions, increase the loss the Investor will incur if they foreclose in its current condition. Environmental issues alone can cause the payoff to fall short, warranting a Short Sale. The Investor can increase their savings over REO by selling the home as a Short Sale. So when the Loss Mitigator or Investor consider reducing the listing or sales price due to these conditions, they are factoring in the extended length of days on the market as an REO.

In most cases the Seller or Agent will need to get 2-3 repair bids from a reputable Contractor. These bids will be used to gauge the amount the Investor will consider as a reduction, or discount, on the sales price. Again, time is money for the Investor.

Water damage Past or present. Water damage can occur from flooding, plumbing, roofing problems, or a variety of other reasons. If the cause of the damage has been repaired with sloppy workmanship, the Investor may consider the "eyesore" as cosmetic. It all depends on the severity of the damage. Make note of dates the damage occurred, and whether the damage was repaired with, or without, an insurance claim. If an insurance claim was filed and paid, chances are the repairs were completed by a professional, and are up to code. However, if repairs were done by the Seller, and /or friends of the Seller, check on whether the repairs were completed within local and State code regulations. If the repairs are not to code, it is possible the home will not pass the Buyer's professional inspection. But, most importantly, the Investor will consider this a problem in selling the home as an REO, since there are usually costs involved to get the property "up to code".

Private individual Investors, or Buyers, are interested in these types of homes since they are usually Contractors by trade. They have financial resources and vendors who can correct the problems inexpensively so they can resale for a profit. The main problem with the Private Investor is they usually "low ball" the price _too_ much. The Loss Mitigator will be using the Investor's value, and your repair bids to determine how much they will adjust on a sales price.

Also, beware of Private Investors who plan to "FLIP" the property. Flipping has become more popular as Short Sales become easier. The

Private Investor offers a below value sales price, and has another Buyer already lined up to "flip" the property to, at closing. Sometimes the property is flipped the very same day the Short Sale closes. Investors are catching onto this practice, so don't get caught up in this kind of mess.

Mold If there was water damage due to flooding, plumbing, roof damage, or standing water in the basement, there may be a potential mold problem for the Investor. The Sellers usually do not have the finances to repair areas affected by these conditions. Obviously, if you see mold or mildew conditions, you will want to take pictures, and note this as a potential issue. The Loss Mitigator will require 2-3 bids to repair by an unbiased Contractor to be considered as an adjustment in the sales price. As discussed in Chapter Six, "*Listing A Short Sale*", potential mold conditions should be mentioned to the Investor's Agent when they arrive to perform their value. The Investor will want to see it noted on both values to verify your claim.

Because mold is a touchy subject these days, the Investor will not want to take the property back at foreclosure. Mold is constantly being challenged by Insurance Companies, nationwide. Most Insurance Companies no longer cover mold evaluation, or restoration. Again, the Investors will consider a lower sales price to avoid moldy properties in their REO inventory.

Fuel tanks (propane or oil). Oil tanks may cause an environmental issue for the Investor. In many US Eastern states, oil is used as heating fuel. Many times these tanks are buried on the lot somewhere. Older tanks can corrode underground, and create a hazardous condition. It is very expensive to correct. They virtually have to dig up the tank, test the ground, and replace contaminated soil. Keep in mind, not all buried tanks are hazardous, though. If the Seller tells you of a known problem, you will want to make sure the Investor's Agent is aware of the issue upon their interior inspection. In most of these cases, the Investor would rather approve a lower the sales price. They do not want to guarantee any repairs on a hazardous property. This is why all Short Sales must be sold in an "as-is" condition.

Propane tanks are usually above ground and can easily be inspected for leaks, or corrosion. Propane is not normally considered an environmental hazard unless you have a unique situation. You will see propane tanks more in rural areas. Whether you are dealing with oil or propane hazards, if it is disclosed by the Seller as a known problem, you must disclose the concern to any potential Buyers. If there is a serious concern, or it is noted in the home inspection, you will need to get two bids from unbiased Contractors. These bids will be required by the Investor before they can give any monetary consideration to the problem.

Foundation problems In most cases, any foundation problems will be obvious to the Seller, Agents, and Buyers. Doors and windows that do not close properly, cracked sheetrock, or concrete gaps and cracks are the most common signs. The Seller may have already had an inspection or repair bid done. Usually the Investor will accept one bid from a reputable Foundation Company, and a copy of the inspection for consideration of reduced sales prices. Again, the Investor will not repair prior to closing.

High line wires The Investor does **not** consider this an environmental issue. Although high line wires are unsightly, there is no real evidence they cause diseases, or health concerns. It is, however, a marketing roadblock. Buyers will want to present a lower offer just because they have to look at the eyesore, and there may be other comparable homes, where they don't. Although this is not a "real" hazard, it should be pointed out to the Investor's Agent as a marketing problem. See if the Investor's Agent will take a picture of the high line wires, which would be included with the Investor's value. This condition could have an impact on the length of a listing, therefore, the Investor may be willing to compromise on sales price, but only slightly. There is no way to attach a devaluation percentage to high line wires.

Roof Repairs or Replacement   If the roof becomes an issue, there may be a chance the Homeowner's Insurance policy will cover the damage. If damaging weather conditions have existed in the past 6 months, ask the Seller to contact their Insurance Company to determine if it is covered under their policy. If the damage is covered, and the mortgage loan is not delinquent, the claim check can be sent to the Seller. But, if the loan is delinquent, or in foreclosure, the Servicer will hold the claim funds, which can be held in escrow for the Buyer. The Investor will likely choose the later option since properties are sold in an "As-Is" condition. If they transfer these funds to the Buyer to repair the roof, they will not reduce the expected sales price based on the damage.

Fire Damage   When a home has sustains fire damage, the Homeowner's Insurance Company, if active, will cover the damage. Again, if the mortgage loan is delinquent, the Servicer will hold the insurance claim check in the Seller's special escrow account. In most cases, the Servicer will want to sell the home in an "As-Is" condition, without repairing the damage.

Depending upon the amount of fire damage, the Investor may request a value on the property as a vacant lot. The cost to repair fire damage often includes demolition, which is very costly. The Investor would have to pay for demolition costs if they took the property back after foreclosure causing an even *larger* loss for them. Private Investor are good Buyers for these situations, but again, the Investor will not let them "low ball" the price because their loss is so high. The estimate from the Insurance Claim Adjustor will be used as your bid to repair.

Of course, if the Seller wants to rebuild and remain in the home, they will need to bring the loan current. The Sellers, if qualified, will be given a choice of the other Alternatives to Foreclosure options. The insurance claim check can be used for the restoration and/or the reinstatement of the loan. No other bids are needed except the Adjustor's estimate.

Other Hazardous Conditions This could be *anything* causing harm, or potential loss to the Buyer. **True Story**: An animal, living in the attic of a home under contract, had built a nest 6 feet around. Believe me, nobody wanted to tango with it. The Investor chose to reduce the sales price by the cost of the extermination. The Buyers were happy about it, and the Short Sale closed. The situations vary and can range from the above story to factory pollution in the air. The Investor will have to consider how it impacts their loss, and the potential for lawsuits filed by the Buyer after closing. Whether they would expect a bid, or not, would depends upon the issue and it's potential harm. Attaching a value to these kinds of issues is almost impossible. Discuss it with the Loss Mitigator for further advice.

Cosmetic repairs The Investor will **not** consider lowering values or sales prices based on cosmetic requests like carpet condition, interior/exterior painting, tile repair or replacement, or updating wallpaper and appliances. These items are almost always noted on the Investor's value and have already been factored into their final value, accordingly. Although cosmetic conditions create a marketing problem, the Investor's consideration on value is minimal. So if the offer is low due to cosmetic repairs, and does not compare to the Investor's value, then the Loss Mitigator will counter the cosmetic repairs out.

NOTES

Chapter Nine

SECOND LIENS

Second liens will be the most common reason for **un**successful Short Sales. Second liens are usually a result of remodeling or credit card debt consolidation loans. Seconds can also be lines of credit, tax liens, judgments, or personal loans. If the lien is based on the home's equity, an appraisal was probably performed when the Second lien originated. As, per my experience, the average difference between the values derived from a Fair Market Value and an Appraisal, is about 15%. This 15% can create a huge gap when Sellers start taking loans out based on their equity. When the home hits a saturated market, the 15% difference can create a Short Sale scenario. Seconds are immediately in a losing position. Lines of credit are similar to credit cards and allow the Seller to pull funds from a maximum approved amount. The current balance of the credit line is the payoff for this type of Second lien.

Liens are listed in the order of their "recording" date on the title. At the foreclosure sale the liens will be paid off in the same order. The power of negotiating the Short Sale approval is also in that order. Since a Short Sale creates a loss, it can affect the First lien, or Second lien, or both! Since the Second is listed in 2nd place on the title, they will be paid whatever is left over after the First lien is paid *in full*! Believe me, the First will make sure they are paid for <u>every</u> fee and expense before giving any left over funds to the Second after the foreclosure sale. So, although, the Second is upset about losing on the loan, they are also realistic enough to realize they have no other choice. The Second can take a grossly reduced settlement, or (possibly) get their entire debt wiped out by the First lien at the foreclosure auction.

The Second lien does not always accept this reasoning. Luckily, more and more Secondary Market Companies are developing Loss Mitigation Departments, giving you a more reasonable, financially educated, decision maker. With*out* the Second's approval to release their lien at closing, your offer will be worthless.

The most likely scenarios are: the First can be paid *in full* from the net proceeds, and the remaining proceeds are short of the Second's payoff. This causes a Short Sale for the Second, only. Or, the First has a Short Sale, and there are no funds left at all for the Second. The First still has to have the Second's approval to close. The First then considers negotiating a settlement with the Second to allow the closing. You must obtain the Second's approval letter, or "Intent to Release" letter, which specifies the approved amount of net proceeds they will accept at closing. This letter also specifies an approved closing date. The approval, or Intent to Release letter, must be on Company letterhead, and be signed and dated.

In either case, the First will possess the power of negotiating since they control the foreclosure action. Occasionally, the Second will initiate a foreclosure, but it is not typical since it furthers their out-of-pocket expenses. Since the First will also incur a loss at foreclosure, they will need to approve a certain amount as a *settlement*, to be paid at closing. The Loss Mitigator for the First will guide you through this negotiation and you will be the messenger. Try to stay neutral and simply relay the counters back and forth until an agreement is reached. Once the First runs their Savings Over REO formulas, they can determine the amount they will offer the Second to settle. The MI Company for the First may also get involved in the countering. So wait for the Loss Mitigator to give you an acceptable amount before you start countering and negotiating with the Second. Or...

The First could be paid in full, but the Second **will not** accept the settlement amount offered by the First. If there are damages or environmental conditions justifying a further loss for the First, or the net proceeds were higher than anticipated by the Investor's value, the First may agree to give a little more to satisfy the Second. Or...

The First may have agreed upon a settlement amount with the Second <u>and</u> another lien, such as a personal loan. It starts to get complicated when there are more than two liens jockeying for position. If the personal loan is in Third position on the title, the chances of them getting anything at foreclosure are slim, to none. But, they can spoil the whole deal by refusing to accept any amount offered by the First. If that were the case, the Second would be approached by the First for the remainder of what the Third is demanding. If the Third still refuses, then the Short Sale could fail. A Second or Third lien can always settle with the Seller outside the closing by allowing them to sign notes, or participate in repayment plans. This gives the Secondary liens the flexibility of approving the Short Sale without having to consider their loan a total loss.

Negotiation skills are the key to Success in Short Sales with Second liens. The most effective approach is to let the other liens know the First lien has intentions of initiating foreclosure and will wipe them all out. If the Second does not want to settle, then the First will move forward with the foreclosure process and take **all** the proceeds from the REO sale to pay themselves off completely. This approach is most effective when a foreclosure sale date has already been set! The liens seem to snap to attention with the mention of "FORECLOSURE". Encourage Secondary liens to take this opportunity to accept the offer, or they will get ***Zip*** in the end (unless there are some little crumbs left over after foreclosure).

Use a reasonable, business-like manner when speaking to them saying such things as, "If the First lien is willing to take a Short Sale based on the Seller's hardship and inability to pay a judgment, why would the Second expect to collect anything from the Seller?" The Second normally ends up writing off the loss, so why wouldn't they want *something*, instead of *nothing*? They usually come around, but it may take some fast dancing for whoever does the negotiating.

The Second will require primarily the same financial package as the First. Make copies of the completed financial package so it can be sent to all liens who are incurring a loss. All liens will want to review the offer, Seller's Net Sheet, and listing agreement, along with the Seller's financial package. Every lien is dealt with individually, and with discretion on your part. But, since the First holds the most weight, you will defer to the First's Loss Mitigator, and let them lead you in the negotiations for a settlement.

The Seller should be the first one to contact the Second lien. The Second may not be aware of the pending foreclosure, and prefer to hear it from the Seller. For some reason, many Sellers will pay their Second lien mortgage and other bills, while falling behind on their First lien mortgage. They don't realize the First lien is usually the only one who will start a foreclosure. For this reason, the Seller should let the Second know about their financial problems from the beginning of the listing. Once the Seller reports a possible default to the Second, you will get a clearer picture of whether they will be willing to settle once an offer is received, or not. If the Seller does not get the answers you need to move forward with the listing, then you may want to step in, and call them yourself.

If Secondary liens will not talk to you, or the Seller, or the First lien's Loss Mitigator, then it is very unlikely they will settle. You can still market the home with the hope the Second will be more willing to communicate once an offer is received. By then, the Second may also be in default, and may be a little more interested in negotiating. As an Agent, being pro-active is commendable, but if the Second refuses to discuss it until an offer is received, don't be discouraged. Actually, this is a positive response. The Second just let you know they are familiar with the Short Sale, and indicated they have an approval process in place. The Second, quite often, does not want the Seller's financial package until an offer is received. The Second may not be as interested in your listing price, and marketing strategies, as the First. They are just interested in the bottom line, which can only be concluded with receipt of an offer.

Another type of Secondary lien is an HOA (Home Owner's Association) with delinquent dues. The HOA does have the ability to refer the account to a Foreclosure Attorney. What most people do not realize is the HOA *precedes* all other liens, except the IRS or Real Estate taxes, in the foreclosure sale. The HOA is notorious for <u>not</u> wanting to negotiate on the amount owed. The Investor is not opposed to paying the HOA as these dues would have to be paid whether on a Short Sale, or at foreclosure sale. The Investor may ask the Seller to pay the delinquent HOA dues from their own pocket, and consider it a contribution towards the Investor's loss. Sometimes the HOA will make special arrangements with the Seller by letting them sign a note or participate in a repayment plan (outside the closing). Or they may take a flat fee at closing to settle their account. Contact the HOA representative, or attorney, to obtain the total amount due.

Since the HOA is typically a local organization, you or the Seller can negotiate directly with the HOA representative. Once negotiations are complete, present the lowest possible settlement amount to the Loss Mitigator for their approval. As with Second liens, the HOA will need to issue a letter of Intent to Release on HOA letterhead. The letter should be signed, dated, and plainly state the settlement amount agreed upon. If the HOA refuses to accept anything less than a full payoff, request a payoff letter from them to present to the Loss Mitigator for review. Whatever the amount, it should be considered a closing cost and appear on your Seller's Net Sheet. See more about the Seller's Net Sheet in Chapter Thirteen, "*The Short Sale Offer*".

So, hang in there, and be patient. These are the hardest Short Sales to close. Many Loss Mitigators do not like to negotiate with Secondary liens. So, it will be to your advantage to make the Short Sale with a Second easier for the First's Loss Mitigator. If you are organized and experienced, you will succeed where others have failed. It can be done!

Chapter Ten

WHAT IS THE MI COMPANY?

So many times there is silence on the other end of the phone when the Mortgage Insurance Company or "MI" Company is mentioned. No... it's not Homeowner's or Hazard Insurance. Actually, it **is** a type of insurance policy. But, this insurance covers the *Investor* on potential losses due to foreclosure, not the Seller. The insurance is usually set up at the loan's origination, and policy premiums are paid monthly through the Seller's escrow account.

To determine if a loan requires MI coverage at origination, the following applies: If the amount of the loan is at, or below 80% LTV (loan to value), there will be no mortgage insurance required. However, if the LTV is higher than 80%, then the MI will be required. If you think about it, you can see why the Investor wants this coverage. There is only a variance from 5-19% (LTV 80% to 95%) loan to value. **Example**: *Sales Price = $200,000 (based on appraisal value) @ 95% LTV = $190,000 loan amount, leaving only $10,000 in equity.* Now, take into account the 15% variance in appraisals, and dropping values (in some areas) = a very slim buffer zone. To make things worse, Sellers are taking out Second liens *against* this equity for debt consolidations, remodeling, and a variety of other reasons.

An inexperienced homeowner may not know they have MI, and may overlook correspondence received from them offering help with the delinquent loan. However, because the name of the MI Company does not appear anywhere on their loan documents or monthly statements, they may not recognize the importance of this correspondence, and throw it away.

As you might imagine, Sellers in foreclosure are bombarded with all kinds of solicitations offering help. They get letters from Realtors, Bankruptcy Attorneys, Debt Consolidation Counselors, Private Investors, Refinance Companies, not to mention the Servicer, and their Attorneys. It is not surprising people are scared, and confused. If they understand who this Other Player is, they will be able to give you the information needed to contact the MI Company directly. Since, in most cases, they will be paying a percentage, or all of the loss via claim, the MI Company will be very interested in discussing the Short Sale with you. The MI Company can be a big influence in the approval process, since the Loss Mitigator must have the MI's approval before a Short Sale approval letter can be issued for closing.

Occasionally, the MI Company solicits defaulted loans with pro-active Loss Mitigation letters. These letters will supply the Sellers with the information they need on the financial package requirements. If the Seller gets correspondence from either the Servicer, or the MI Company, take the opportunity to establish a direct line to the "decision maker". Encourage your Seller to initiate contact, and fax a copy of your *Seller's Authorization Form.*

In most cases, the MI Company representative will discuss the required documents needed to review your offers. However, be warned, most

Servicers will not disclose the name, or number of the MI Company. Even with a *Seller's Authorization Form*, the Loss Mitigator will protect the MI from an onslaught of anxious Sellers, Buyers, Agents, etc.

There are two forms of MI coverage; Primary and Pool. Both types must approve any Short Sale losses, and issue approvals to the Loss Mitigator. Each loan is set up different. Some loans have only primary insurance; some, only pool. And, some loans have *both*. Short Sale offers must either be reviewed and approved by the MI Company, or a Servicer who has delegated authority to approve on the MI's and Investor's behalf.

Delegated authority is becoming more common everyday and gives the Servicer authority to approve losses within certain parameters. If the losses fall outside the parameters, the entire financial package, listing agreement, Seller's Net Sheet, and offer must be submitted directly to the MI Company. Their in-house Loss Mitigators will review and evaluate the Savings Over REO they can expect from your offer. The financial package can be sent to them, or the Servicer's Loss Mitigation Department. They usually work together on the approval process.

To estimate which Players will lose, and *how much* they will lose, use the following examples. These examples are based on conventional, single lien, mortgage loans. The amount of loss the MI Company will pay in a claim is determined by the **Total Debt** of the loan (balance, delinquent interest, escrow balance, corporate advances, inspection, legal fees, etc) multiplied by the % of MI coverage = Claim Amount. The percentage of coverage may be 12%, 25%, 35%, or any place in between. ***Example: Total Debt $100,000.00 X 25% primary MI coverage = $25,000.00 maximum loss MI will cover.***

If the loss does not exceed the percentage of MI coverage, then the Investor will not incur a loss. You will only need approval from the MI Company, who will issue their approval letter to the Loss Mitigator. The Loss Mitigator then issues an approval letter for closing without having to obtain any approvals from the Investor. After all, since the Investor was covered by the MI policy, they will not have a loss. ***Example: Total Debt $225,000.00 X 25% primary MI coverage = $56,250.00 maximum coverage. Net Short Sale Proceeds $186,000 - Total Debt $225,000.00 = $39,000.00 loss, which falls within the 25% MI coverage with no loss to the Investor.***

The other type of MI coverage is pool insurance. The pool insurance is similar to primary, except the pool MI Company covers any additional losses over, and above, the primary insurance coverage, up to 100%. ***Example: Net proceeds $180,000.00 – Total Debt $250,000.00 = $70,000.00 loss; Total Debt $250,000.00 X 25% primary MI coverage = $62,500.00 max coverage; Short Sale Loss - $70,000.00 - $62,500.00 primary MI coverage = $7,500.00 pool MI coverage loss.*** In the preceding example, the lower the net proceeds, the higher the loss for the pool MI insurer, all the way up to a 100% of a Total Debt payoff. Whether the loan has both primary and pool, or just pool coverage, there will be no loss for the Investor. Loans having only primary can still result in a loss for the Investor if the loss exceeds the primary's percentage of coverage.

If a Second is being paid out of the net proceeds from the offer, the amount paid would increase the loss for the MI Company and/or Investor. It is reasonable why they would want to have a say in the amount to be paid to the Second lien at closing. Since most Loss Mitigators do not have delegation to approve a VA Short Sale, they work directly with the VA representative. The financial package will be sent from the Servicer to VA where their representatives will review the offer, and either approve or deny it. FHA loans are insured by HUD, also known as the US Department of Housing and Urban Development. HUD acts as the MI Company and incurs losses at foreclosure. HUD has given most Servicers delegated authority to approve a Short Sale, making the process much easier than VA. Both VA and FHA have websites to help determine where to call for help.

Most MI Companies will require the loan be at least 30 days delinquent before they will consider a Short Sale. There are times, though, when the default is considered "imminent" and they will look at offers before the loan is delinquent. So, if there are reasons, like illness or death, go ahead and send the financial package to the Loss Mitigator. Most Loss Mitigators specialize in either conventional or government loans, so be sure to specify which type of loan you are calling about when you contact the Loss Mitigation Department.

Each MI Company is different in their approach, but they all share a common interest – sell the home as a Short Sale if they will lose more at the foreclosure sale. The MI's accumulated claim loss basically stops on the day the home forecloses. So they will consider all the factors such as the length of foreclosure in your State, how long in foreclosure already, property condition, and the Seller's ability to pay either cash towards the loss, or sign a note. The amount of the note they offer is usually a calculated percentage of the loss. The notes are unsecured, interest free, and can be spread over a 5, 7 or 10 year terms. If the Sellers state they cannot sign a note for the requested amount; ask them to make a counter on the term, or amount offered by the MI or Loss Mitigator.

The Seller must justify why they are unable to sign a note, or pay cash, for the requested terms. The worst thing a Seller can do is flatly refuse to sign a note, without any negotiations. Sometimes it works, but most of the time the MI Company digs in their heels, and will not budge. If the Seller is aware of this before hand, then they will not over react when it happens. Hopefully they will be able to negotiate a settlement successfully.

Remember, the MI Company has the Seller's financial package. They have a pretty good idea of who can, and cannot, afford to contribute. The MI Company does not usually make a habit of asking for cash, or notes from Sellers who do not have the ability to pay. The Loss Mitigator may leave you out of this discussion altogether, and go directly to the Sellers with the MI Company's "contribution" request. The MI Company has the final say, though, so tread carefully. If the Seller agrees to sign a note at closing, the note is sent to the Closing Company, and signed with other closing documents; or sent directly to the Seller's home prior to closing.

The MI Company works directly with the Servicer's Loss Mitigator. The Loss Mitigator in turn, corresponds with the Agents and Sellers. When the MI Company issues an approval or denial, it is sent to the Servicer, only. The Loss Mitigator will be responsible for obtaining all MI approvals, both primary and pool. If, however, there is no pool coverage for loss that exceeds the primary coverage, the Loss Mitigator has to obtain approval from the Investor for the remaining shortage. Again, if the Loss Mitigator has delegated authority, they may be able to approve the loss on behalf of the Investor, which speeds up the approval process greatly. The Loss Mitigator will not issue an approval letter until **all** approvals are received from the Investor, MI Company's), and/or Secondary liens.

Chapter Eleven

MY SELLER HAS FILED BANKRUPTCY

You may be working with a Seller who has filed bankruptcy. If they have not yet filed, try to discourage them from doing so until they have exhausted all their options. Bankruptcy is sometimes necessary to relieve the Seller from excessive debts, but the Seller can always file the bankruptcy after the home is sold. Commonly, Sellers will file a bankruptcy to stop the foreclosure sale, which can be a useful stalling tactic. But bankruptcy may be unnecessary if you have an offer on the property, and the foreclosure sale date has been set. Ask the Loss Mitigator to postpone the sale date to allow you time to close on the offer. If they approve the postponement, you will have saved the Seller from bankruptcy, *and* years of blemished credit. As previously addressed, there could be a cost to the Seller to postpone the sale, but it is up to the discretion of the Investor to determine if, or how much, the Seller pays.

Unfortunately, most Sellers file bankruptcy as soon as financial problems arise, and before you have a chance to explain the Short Sale option. They do not realize the foreclosure in their State could take up to 12 months, giving them ample time to pursue other avenues to cure their financial situation. You can use this time to get the home listed, and closed. Since most Short Sales only take about 3-6 months from start to finish, you should have plenty of time to close (except in short foreclosure States). Refer to *Foreclosure Time Table* on page 26. The key is to find Sellers before they file, and/or before the foreclosure starts. It's not always possible, though. So the following are explanations of how to handle Sellers already in bankruptcy.

Most Bankruptcy Attorneys are in favor of the Short Sale because the Seller can be relieved of financial responsibility for the home and the 1099 capital gain consequences. Attorneys feel the largest benefit for their clients is the relief of the 1099. This is something even *they* cannot offer their clients. But the Short Sale CAN!

When the Seller files a **Chapter 7 bankruptcy**, any pending Short Sale offers cannot close until the bankruptcy is "discharged". The discharge is actually a legal motion filed by the Bankruptcy Attorney through the courts. Once the bankruptcy is discharged, the Seller will no longer owe any of the debts they included in the bankruptcy. They have been "discharged" from debt; but only unsecured debt. What some Sellers do not realize is that secured debts, like the house and car, are not *completely* forgiven. Basically, (in plain language): "unsecured" debts like credit cards, can be discharged, and no further debt is owed. With "secured" debts like the house, the delinquent amount of the debt may be discharged, but the remaining balance is still due, and payable. The Sellers can "reaffirm" the secured debts, and continue with payments to keep their home. However, if they do not make payments, the house will be taken back by the Investor by starting up the foreclosure again.

Since the bankruptcy stops the foreclosure on the day of the filing, the Servicer will have the right to start pushing forward with their attempts to foreclose once the proper motions are filed. The Foreclosure Attorney for the Servicer will file a Motion for Relief and "Lift of Stay". This means the protection from foreclosure is "lifted" from the secured debt; the home. The problem with the Chapter 7 bankruptcy, in relation to the Short Sale, is since no offers can be approved for closing until the Seller is discharged from debt, the Lift of Stay may be granted *before* the debt is discharged. There could be an overlapping period of time in which the Seller is unable to close on the Short Sale because the discharge has not been received yet, and the home could foreclose in the meantime. Of course, this is deadly to the Short Sale.

If you can get a copy of the discharge notice from the Seller, or their Bankruptcy Attorney, you can then proceed with your Short Sale closing. You may continue your listing before the discharge, but if you get an offer, you will not be able to present it for approval. So, it is best if you stop, or at least slow down, your marketing until the discharge is received.

Now for the UP side...The Short Sale for a discharged Seller is almost *guaranteed* to be approved since the Investor will not legally be able to pursue a judgment on the loss. Additionally, the Seller will not be required to submit a financial package, sign a note, or pay a cash contribution for part of the loss at closing. Timing is the key. The only exception here is VA, who will require the Seller to reaffirm their debt before they will approve a Short Sale on a discharged Chapter 7.

A Reaffirmation Agreement is sent by the Servicer to the Seller's Bankruptcy Attorney. It is a request, or agreement, to reaffirm the debt on the mortgage, only. If the Seller signs, and returns this letter, they are basically stating their willingness to keep the home and continue to make their payments. If the loan is delinquent, the Servicer will investigate other options to help the Seller bring the account current. Reaffirmation could back fire if the Seller tries to keep the loan current, but again falls behind. The foreclosure would then be started all over again, and the Sellers would be unprotected from the Servicer's efforts to collect, or foreclose.

A possible Short Sale killer is the **Chapter 13 bankruptcy**. As you may be aware, this bankruptcy places the Seller on a court monitored payment plan for their debts. The court will assign a Trustee to collect the monthly payments for all the debts, except for *secured* debts, such as the home and car. These secured debts would have to be paid by the Seller, outside the bankruptcy plan. So if the Seller does not start to make regular payments to the Servicer during the bankruptcy plan, the Servicer will file a Motion for Relief, and start up the foreclosure, again.

If the Sellers pay their mortgage payments, the Servicer will keep the foreclosure on "hold", or cancel it to avoid further legal fees. You can market the home during the Chapter 13, but if you get an offer, you will need the court's approval to close. If you decide to get the court's approval, you will need to contact the Trustee of the Chapter 13 plan. The Trustee may need to obtain their own value and payoff before they can issue their approval. As you might guess, this can delay your counter back to the Buyers.

Again, Bankruptcy Attorneys are normally in favor of the Short Sale option, even on a Chapter 13. If the bankruptcy is "dismissed" because the Sellers did not make the "court required" payments to the Trustee, all the debts involved will automatically be due, and payable again. Supply the dismissal letter from the courts to the Loss Mitigator, and they will move forward with the Short Sale. But, be forewarned, if the Chapter 13 is dismissed, the Servicer will probably start up the foreclosure again immediately upon notification. If the Seller stays in the Chapter 13 payment plan, and makes the payments to the Servicer, they will eventually be "discharged" from debt. This process can take up to 5 years! So my best advice is to avoid the Chapter 13 bankruptcy Seller, if possible.

If the Sellers are adamant about pursuing Chapter 13, be sure to let them know they have the option to list the property if the bankruptcy is dismissed. Then they can call you to list their home if they are unable to perform on the court required payment plan. Most Loss Mitigators will require the Seller's financial package, or Chapter 13 bankruptcy plan. Since the "dismissed" Seller is no longer protected by bankruptcy, they will need to show their *inability* to maintain mortgage payments any longer to qualify for the Short Sale option.

You will very seldom deal with a Seller involved in a **Chapter 11 bankruptcy**. This type of bankruptcy is more for business failures. Occasionally they show up, though, because more, and more, Sellers are self-employed. **True Story** - An Agent had listed four high-dollar properties, all included in the Seller's Chapter 11 bankruptcy. The homes had been listed for over a year and had been through two other Agents before he listed them. Since the homes were involved in the bankruptcy, the foreclosure action was on hold - for over a year! The accrued daily interest alone caused the homes to sell as Short Sales. The payoffs had increased enormously. The Investor knew they were going to lose - one way, or the other.

Knowing the bankruptcy could continue for an extended amount of time, they were very accommodating and willing to "stop the bleeding". The payoff continued to get higher every day - on all *four* properties. Luckily, an experienced Short Sale Agent stepped in, and within 30 days he had his first offer. The other three homes quickly followed with offers, and closings. Believe me; this Agent was extremely happy when all four Short Sales closed within a 6 month period. His commission was five figures on each deal! It wasn't easy, and he took a lower commission percentage, but because he knew the Short Sale process, he was able to get all these homes released from the bankruptcy proceedings, and approved by the Investor and/or MI Companies.

The Seller's attorney was thrilled because his client was released from the tax consequences, which would have followed the foreclosure. You see, the credit report and the forgiveness of debt were not as important to this Seller, but the capital gains on losses ranging in the area of $400,000 would have followed him for years to come. You, too, can find these gems!

Again, I emphasize that I am not an Attorney or Accountant. I suggest you consult legal counsel if you have further questions. The information in this chapter was derived through my experience as a Loss Mitigator.

Chapter Twelve

MY SELLER IS DECEASED

Another source for Short Sales is the deceased Seller. Obviously, this is a terrible time for the family of the deceased. This is the time for your compassionate side to emerge. If you have ever lost a loved one, you know the family is not thinking straight about *anything*, but their loss. You can aid them in their time of need just by offering your help when they need it.

Let them know there are options available from the Investor. These options will help them deal with the financial side of their grief. Of course, be respectful, and give the family time to sort things out. Maybe just send a card or flyer to the home of the deceased, offering your advice on their dilemma. It takes a special kind of Agent to approach the grieving family, so by all means, do not contact them too soon after the funeral. Most family members, or their attorneys, will make contact with the Servicer sooner, or later. OK, as you know by now, I am not an Attorney, or a CPA. The information you are about to read is taken from my years of experience in approving Short Sales for major US Investors. It is recommend you seek legal advice on any questions you may have about probate, or the asset liquidation process.

Having someone to sign on behalf of the Seller is very important. Without it, no listing, offer, or closing can occur. If there is no authorized signer, or legal executor, you will have a losing battle. Establish who will sign before moving forward with *your* time and money. There are times when it just won't work, and the Servicer is forced to proceed with foreclosure.

If relatives wish to take over the mortgage payments, there is an option called an "assumption". The assumption is basically modifying the terms of the loan, releasing the deceased from title, while adding the family member (s) onto the title. You can help the family by supplying them with a financial package and guidance in applying for the assumption. The family member, who intends on assuming the payments, must qualify and show the ability to make payments. Bottom line on the assumption is; you will not get a listing, because there is no need for a Real Estate Agent on this option. You can, however, take satisfaction in knowing you helped someone when times were tough. And, you never know; they may return to you for the listing, short or not, if they do not qualify for the assumption.

On the other hand, if the family members wish to sell the home (with equity), the listing and closing would be like any other listing and closing with a deceased Seller. If you have never closed a sale with a deceased Seller, it can be sized up for you short, and sweet: Start by obtaining a *certified* copy of the death certificate and the name/# of the attorney, or Trustee of Probate, or a family representative (usually assigned by the Will, Attorney, or Courts). Fax the death certificate to the Servicer so they will stop Collections, and foreclosure. (They waste money on these efforts to bring the account current.) Get the Closer from the Closing Company and the representative for the deceased together, and you are set! They should work out everything else between themselves. You just made an important connection, which assures a successful closing. You may have to jump in to help occasionally, but mainly just make sure the Closer and representative continue to communicate until the closing is completed. The Short Sale, however, applies only if there is **no** equity, and the family members are either uninterested, or unqualified, for the assumption. If there is a probate open, the Servicer will put the mortgage account on hold until the probate is complete, or the home is released. This will give you more time to analyze the Short Sale possibilities, and market the home before it becomes vulnerable to foreclosure, again.

In a probate, the assets and liabilities of the deceased are calculated to determine who, and how, all the debts will be paid. When there are not enough assets to cover all the debts (including the home with negative equity), the Short Sale is the answer. No financial package will be required. But, as previously stated, you will need a certified copy of the death certificate to submit to the Loss Mitigation Department as proof of hardship. The Loss Mitigator may also request an accounting of assets from the probate. The Investor is usually very accommodating in approving these Short Sales, but they may want to review this accounting to be sure their loss is justified. If there are funds left over, after liquidating all assets in probate, the Investor would expect to receive those funds at closing to help decrease their loss. Very seldom do they push this point, though.

There is a possibility the deceased Seller had Life Insurance coverage on their loan. If this is the case, the Short Sale may not be necessary. The Life Insurance sometimes pays off the remaining mortgage debt, depending on the policy, and premium status. Beware though, occasionally when a home is refinanced, the Seller is not aware the Life Insurance coverage they previously had was not transferred to the new loan. The Loss Mitigator will be able to check on the insurance status, you just have to ask.

Homes from the deceased Seller are far, and few between, but worth a shot. In most cases, there is either equity, or family members take over the payments. But, occasionally, the home is in need of your Short Sale expertise. Be ready if the need arises.

Chapter Thirteen

THE SHORT SALE OFFER

Congratulation! You have your first Short Sale offer. Let's get started on the right foot. In this chapter you will learn how to avoid costly mistakes, and how to get your Short Sale reviewed, First!

Don't let the number of Players boggle your mind. Decide which ones are the most important for obtaining your Short Sale approval. Use the information from the *Seller's Questionnaire,* and form an outline of who's playing. The first Player will <u>always</u> be the Loss Mitigator for the First lien. Since the First is usually larger than most other liens, they are more likely to be in a position of loss. Also remember, the First is commonly the initiator of the foreclosure action. So, whether the First will fall short, or not, you will want to notify them of the pending offer. Now add Players based on the number of liens involved. Determine if the First lien will fall short of a total payoff, and then move down the list of other liens, deducting their payoffs from the estimated net proceeds until the proceeds become a negative number. Once you hit a negative, that lien will incur a loss. If the Second lien falls short, their Loss Mitigator is placed in position after the First lien.

"Estimated" net proceeds can be figured by subtracting the anticipated Seller's closing costs (include your commission, concessions, repairs, and any other lien payoffs) from the sales price. If there are proceeds remaining after subtracting **all** payoffs; It is not a Short Sale. Refer to Chapter Nine "*Second Liens*" for suggestions on negotiating a Short Sale settlement with Secondary liens. Only worry about those Players who will incur a loss. Once you have whittled it down to the main Player, you can focus on them for your Short Sale approval.

If the loan is in foreclosure, and a sale date has been set for the auction, the First's Loss Mitigator can request a foreclosure postponement to allow you time to get approvals, and close the sale. Some Loss Mitigators are delegated with the Investor to approve a 30 day postponement of the auction date, but will need to obtain approval from the Investor for any future postponements.

Each Investor has their own set of criteria for their review of your offer. The Loss Mitigator will review on behalf of the Investor. The denial, or approval, will be based on the Seller's hardship reason, financial ability to pay/not pay, and the Seller's willingness to *participate* by signing documents at closing. Without the Seller's full participation in submitting financial information and signing, the Investor will deny the offer. And, they will probably not entertain any future offers until the Seller does participate completely. The Loss Mitigator will be a liaison between your Seller and the Investor. Although, most Agents participate on behalf of their Sellers. By working directly with the Loss Mitigator, you will avoid miscommunication of any countering, or closing instructions.

Now, how do you get the Loss Mitigator to look at your offer "First"? Send them everything they need for their review, and follow-up with phone calls, and emails. The Loss Mitigator will appreciate your complete Short Sale package more than you know. The complete package consists of the following: Seller's financial statement, hardship letter with any documents substantiating the "reason" for the default, pay stubs (1 full month), bank statements (3 months), tax returns for the past two years. If the Sellers are self-employed, they will need to also include Schedules C and/or E of their tax returns. These schedules can also be used as the self-employed Seller's income average, in lieu of pay stubs. They will require a fax (yes, fax is acceptable) of the listing agreement, your value (with supporting comps), the offer (Subject to Investor Approval and sold As-Is), and the Seller's Net Sheet (includes all Seller costs at closing).

This brings us to a very important point for Success in Short Sales. Make sure all incoming offers are **"Subject to Investor Approval"** *and* sold in an **"As-Is"** condition. These clauses must be inserted in the "Other Conditions" or "Addendum" part of your standard Real Estate contract. Being aware of this requirement upfront will help you avoid going back to the Buyers, and their Agent, to have the offer changed, and initialed. This back and forth countering often results in a stressful sale under any conditions. Since there may be a delay in responding to their offer, it's best to do this up front.

The "Subject to Investor Approval" clause basically means the signed offer, or contract, is void without the Investor's approval for a reduced payoff. You see, the sales price and the Seller's closing costs are now subject to countering and/or adjusting. You, or the Seller, are no longer making the decisions. You are simply relaying the Loss Mitigator's counters to the Buyer and their Agent. Do not give the Buyer the contact #'s for the Loss Mitigator. The calls and emails do nothing, but slow down the process of approval.

This clause can also save you, and the Seller, from legal consequences, like Breach of Contract. When the Seller signs an offer which does not pay off all loan balances, the Buyer can claim the Sellers were aware of the shortage. Unless the Sellers had intentions of bringing the shortage to closing in cash, they would need the Investor to "approve" the shortage. The Seller could be held liable for expenses incurred by the Buyers, while awaiting an answer to their offer. Protect your Seller, and yourself, by including the "Subject to Investor Approval" clause in all listings and offers.

There are times when offers come in, already signed by the Sellers. Call the Buyer's Agent, and explain why you are sending them an addendum to the offer to be "Subject to Investor Approval". The addendum needs to be initialed, and dated by the Buyers. This is a good time to discuss the Short Sale process with the Buyer's Agent, including a possible delay in countering. This should help keep everyone calm during the approval process. The Loss Mitigator may be able to estimate of how long it will take to get the response from the Investor, or MI Company. Just ask. The MI Companies and Investors are usually very interested in getting you an answer as quickly as possible. Time is Money for them, too.

The "As-Is" clause is required to avoid any responsibility of the Investor on the condition of the property. For this reason, most Investors will not approve the cost for a Home Warranty Plan in the closing costs. It can give the "impression" the property is warranted. The Investor does not want to have any further dealings with the property after the day of closing.

The "As-Is" clause does not necessarily mean you cannot allow repairs. As discussed earlier, be sure the requested repairs have a value impact on the resale of the property as an REO. The Investor's main advantage in the

Short Sale is to increase their Saving Over REO. So, if you can show substantiation as to why the Investor would rather adjust the sales price in lieu of the repair, they will realize the monetary value of selling the property now, instead of later.

They will reject, or counter out, any "cosmetic" items such as carpet allowances, interior/exterior paint, fixture replacements, or any other repairs not having a structural, or hazardous consequences. Keep in mind, the Loss Mitigator is reviewing the condition of the property via the Investor's value. This value will note any damage or repairs seen on the day of their initial inspection. The value will also have an estimate of repair costs. If damage occurred after the Investor's value was performed, supply photos and estimates to repair to the Loss Mitigator. They understand these situations can arise. In most cases, they would rather adjust the value down, than make the repair. See more information on how to handle special situations in Chapter Fourteen *"Contingencies, and Other Contract Requirements"*.

If you choose to spend your own money on repairs, you will most likely not be reimbursed at closing. Very seldom does the Investor reimburse Agents for expenses incurred during the listing, no matter what the reason. If the home needs to be winterized or secured in any way, call the Loss Mitigator. They have resources to order these property preservation items through the Servicer at minimal expense.

If you plan to pursue reimbursement at closing for a particular repair expense, be ready with receipts. Be able to justify why the expenses were *absolutely* necessary. If you had the utilities turned on, and you paid the deposit, they will **not** pay. If you had a cleaning crew make the property ready for showings, they will **not** pay. If you watered and mowed the yard during the listing, they will **not** pay. But, if you repaired a roof leak to prevent further interior damage, and you have a receipt, they **may consider** reimbursing you at closing because you were preserving the value of the property. If you paid for a Hazardous Material Inspection (mold, asbestos, underground propane or gas tanks, or other hazardous situations), they *may* **reimburse** you at closing. But, in all cases, you should ask the Loss Mitigator, first.

Next, prepare the Seller's Net Sheet to submit with your offer to the Loss Mitigator. This net sheet will itemize all the possible closing costs for the *Seller* at closing. It is better to overestimate, than underestimate. Since the Investor will be determining their net proceeds from this net sheet, it is best to get the closing costs from the Title, or Closing Company. Review the offer closely to be sure you have included any "Other" items noted in the contract. These items are usually Buyer's closing cost concessions, points on the Buyer's loan, reimbursements, and repair allowances. Because the Loss Mitigator and Investors use these net sheets to determine the reduced payoff amount for the approval letter, it's in your best interest to contact a Closer for a preliminary HUD Settlement Statement. Avoid changes on the approval letter by obtaining the correct closing costs for the Seller *before* submitting your net sheet to the Loss Mitigator.

Typically, Buyers want an answer to their offer quickly. Let them know the response from your Seller may be delayed by a week, or two. Of course, the length of the delay will depend upon the Investor, the Servicer, the MI Company, and/ or the Loss Mitigator for each lien involved. Ask the Seller to immediately order a payoff from all liens with a "good through" date, approximately three weeks from the date of the offer. The payoff will have a *per diem,* or per day, amount on it. This amount can be added to, or subtracted from, the total payoff amount based on the closing date and the "good through" date. Payoffs from the Servicer can take a long time, so ask the Seller to request it from their Servicer, "in writing" as soon as possible. Once you have the payoff, you will be able to verify the amount of the shortage.

One major "No-No" is submitting offers from blood relatives of Sellers who are currently in foreclosure. Blood relatives are typically considered parents, siblings, and children. This is called an "Arms Length Transaction". The Investor frowns upon selling to anyone who will transfer the property back to the Seller. Simply put, the Seller cannot retain the property in a Short Sale. If you think the offer may be from a relative, disclose this to the Loss Mitigator. There are times when they may be willing to consider having the Buyer submit a notarized "Arms Length Transaction" letter specifically stating the Buyer has no intention of returning the property to the Seller after closing.

OK, you are now ready to submit the offer to the Loss Mitigator or Secondary liens. All liens involved in the Short Sale need a copy of the offer, Seller's Net Sheet, listing agreement (with reductions), and the Seller's financial package. Again, faxing is acceptable. Make a follow-up call to those Players who are approving the Short Sale to be sure all faxes were received.

The delay starts Now! It takes time for the Loss Mitigator to get your offer submitted and approved by the Investor, or MI Company. So, as soon as you receive an offer – call the Loss Mitigator! They prefer you not counter until they have reviewed the offer first. So no matter how outrageously low the offer is, present it to the Loss Mitigator. They will let you know how high they want to counter. This is when the "good guy/bad guy" negotiations start. The approval process, baring there are no complications, can take approximately 1-2 weeks.

Once you have received approval letters or letters of Intent to Release from all liens incurring a loss, you are ready to set your date for closing. If the dates or net proceeds change, **each** approval letter will need to be changed to match. With experience, you will learn how to coordinate this process efficiently.

Chapter Fourteen

CONTINGENCIES & OTHER CONTRACT REQUIREMENTS

Contingencies often show up in offers. If the contingencies are for such items like refrigerators, stoves, curtains, etc., they are not a concern for the Investor. These decisions are made by the Agents and Sellers, just as in any normal transaction. The contingencies affecting the net proceeds, like cash to the Buyers for closing costs, carpet replacement, or cosmetic repairs, do concern the Investor. Most of the time these issues can be resolved by countering, or increasing/decreasing the sales price to allow the contingency to remain.

The Investor will not, however, allow a contingency for the Buyers to sell their home first. This kind of contingency will need to either be countered out, or you will need to use this offer as a backup. The Loss Mitigator will require proof of the Buyer's home closing before they will approve the offer with this type of contingency. If the Buyer's home closing has been set, you can show proof by faxing the Buyer's loan commitment letter (not pre-approval letter) and a copy of the HUD settlement statement showing the date the Buyer's home is due to close. Many Agents will place this type of contingent offer as a backup, giving them the ability to continue marketing for more desirable offers.

Once you have addressed the contingencies, whether they are resolved or not, go ahead and submit the offer to the Loss Mitigator. An experienced Loss Mitigator will be able to determine the advantage, or disadvantage, of considering an adjusted sales price, but don't leave it all up to them. If you really want this offer, with contingencies, fight for it!

Be creative, and communicate clearly the reasons why the Investor does **not** want to foreclose on this home. Be sure to ask the Loss Mitigator to postpone the foreclosure if an auction date is pending. If the savings to the Investor are not out weighed by the cost of the foreclosure postponement, the Investor will approve it. But, if the Buyer does not have a contract on their home yet, the Investor will not postpone the foreclosure sale. There would be no way for them to gauge the amount of time to postpone since it would be dependent upon an unknown factor. If you counter out certain items prior to submitting the offer to the Investor, you may cause duplicate countering. Or, the Investor may counter something you didn't. This creates a back and forth scenario, which is frustrating for everyone. So, when countering, be sure you update your net sheet and have changes in the offer initialed.

The most effective negotiating tactic is known as the "Good Guy/Bad Guy" part of the game. The Investor, or Loss Mitigator, always plays the "Bad" Guy. The Investor usually counters out any contingencies, so you get to play the "Good" Guy. It is recommended you let the Buyers know which items may be affected upon your initial review of the offer. This will prepare them for the counter with no unexpected surprises. Since you and the Sellers are not in control of this process, you will be in the middle. But, it's not a bad place to be. At this point in the game, you are siding with the Investor, and relaying counters to the Buyer.

The game is about to get fun! Good Guy/Bad Guy negotiating has been around forever. It is very effective because it takes the pressure off of you and steers the Buyer's tension towards the Investor, an unknown Player. This is another reason why you do not supply the name/# of your contact at the Servicer to the Buyer. Work out your specific roles with the Loss Mitigator, who will be negotiating on behalf of the Investor, or the MI Company. The Loss Mitigator will counter out everything they can to avoid further loss. They are going to be interested in numbers, not hurt feelings. If you plan on negotiating contingencies with the Loss Mitigator, you will take on the "Good Guy" role (the Buyer is the "Bad Guy").

It sounds like you are playing both sides of the coin, Right? Well, you are. You have to be able to communicate your points of negotiation as it applies to each Player. The Buyer wants a good deal on the home, the Seller wants to get out of this without any repercussions, the Loss Mitigator wants to show the Investor and MI Company the highest amount of Savings Over REO, and you want your commission.

Unfortunately, the Investor's philosophy is "if the offer falls through there will be another one just around the corner". And, they are usually right. Since you have the home priced right, the offers will keep rolling in. They will review as many offers as you receive prior to the foreclosure sale.

NOTES

Chapter Fifteen

NEGOTIATION POINTERS

The negotiations include the countering of the sales price and closing costs, and will be initiated by the Loss Mitigator of whichever lien is at a loss. The majority of Loss Mitigators are experienced negotiators. They negotiate on behalf of the Investor, the MI Company, or Private Investors everyday. *Everything* is negotiable. The Loss Mitigator will review the sales price, value, closing costs, and commissions.

The sales price will be countered to, or above, the Investor's value sales price. Most of the time their counters will not be out of line, but sometimes the value can be "off" causing the Loss Mitigator to counter too high. Go ahead, and relay the counter to the Buyer, anyway. Tell the Buyers you are an innocent bystander and can only relay their counter back to the Loss Mitigator. After all, you are not trying to run the Buyers off, but still have to counter to the sales price requested by the Loss Mitigator. Take the Buyer's counter back to the Loss Mitigator. The Investor, or MI Company, might actually be the ones negotiating through the Loss Mitigator, so they may not have much control over the counters. The Loss Mitigator is simply relaying the counters requested by the Investor. So don't "shoot the messenger". The Agent is usually stuck in the middle. As mentioned in Chapter Fourteen, *Contingencies, and Other*

Contract Requirements use the "Good Guy/Bad Guy" game to help relieve some of the pressure. The Agent gets to be the "Good Guy", and the Investor is the "Bad Guy". However, do not give access to the Loss Mitigator to the Buyer, or their Agent. The Loss Mitigator will expect you to keep everyone calm during the negotiations.

If the First lien is paid off in full with the net proceeds from the sale, the negotiations will start with the Second lien. The Seller will start the negotiations with Second and Other liens, but the First lien Loss Mitigator may have to step in if the Second's settlement amount creates a shortfall for the First.

The most effective point of negotiation to use on the Second will be the foreclosure. Since their lien can be "wiped out" at foreclosure, they may consider taking a lesser amount to settle. If the foreclosure sale date has already been set, you will have a great deal of leverage. The Second will want to get as much of their outstanding balance as possible. Keep in mind, though, the Investor or MI Company will only be willing to pay them a reduced payoff amount. The negotiations may start out as low as $1,000! If there are enough net proceeds to pay a larger amount, it will be figured, to the penny. If the Second does not accept the maximum amount offered (without putting the First at a further loss), the Short Sale could fall through.

This would be a good time to mention any environmental issues or damage to the property. The First might consider a larger loss up front to avoid taking the property back into their REO Inventory. Environmental Issues can cause a higher loss to the First lien after foreclosure due to an extended marketing time as an REO. The Loss Mitigator will use a

Savings Over REO formula to determine the amount of Investor loss with, and without the Second's reduced payoff. They will also review the Savings Over REO before, and after the foreclosure. The Investor's decision to approve will be based on these figures.

This Short Sale formula is a concoction of percentages and balances, which help the Loss Mitigator review the best case, and worst case, scenarios. All Investors have their own systems to calculate their Savings Over REO. It takes into account the value, sales price, other lien payoffs, Seller's closing costs, total First lien debt payoff, foreclosure costs, condition of the property, and marketing conditions, by State. Knowing this, you may be able to hit upon some of the Investor's hot points during this phase of the game. If you can attach a value to conditions of the home, they will be more interested in your position, because it affect's their savings, in the long run.

An approval letter from the First lien will replace the need for a payoff at closing and will most likely come from the Loss Mitigator. If the loss is taken by the Second, you will need a letter of "Intent to Release" on their letterhead, signed and dated. Letters of "Intent to Release" will also be needed from any other Secondary liens, like HOA, lines of credit, tax liens (including the IRS), and personal loans. The letter of "Intent to Release" will need to include the negotiated reduced payoff, and wiring instructions for closing.

There can be a variety of liens that show up on the Title Search. Attachments to the property like a water softener, or hot tub, can be removed from the home, and returned. These vendors will usually release without any compensation. An in-ground pool, on the other hand, cannot be given back. The pool would need to be negotiated as a lien, and will require a letter of "Intent to Release". A lien created by the previous owners for the down payment or Buyer financing will also need to be negotiated and released. The Seller should contact the Secondary liens. Their participation is needed here since other Secondary liens may not be willing to discuss the account with anyone, but the Sellers.

Delinquent HOA dues often need to be paid in full, including their legal fees. There are occasions when they will agree to a settlement amount, or a repayment plan with the Seller, outside the closing. Since the HOA can initiate foreclosure <u>ahead</u> of the Servicer, and get paid in full, they are more difficult to negotiate. The Servicer knows this, and should be helpful in negotiating the best possible settlement.

There are only a few types of liens that *supersede* the First lien mortgage. The IRS, the HOA and the taxing authorities for the City, County, or State will be paid after the foreclosure sale by the Investor. This means the Investor will usually take the property back at foreclosure, and will have to pay off these types of liens to get clear title for the resale of the home as an REO. On "escrowed mortgages", the Servicer is responsible for keeping the Real Estate taxes current, but they are usually unaware if HOA dues are delinquent.

Whereas, the IRS does not initiate foreclosures, and has been very willing to work with the Sellers on delinquent IRS taxes, the HOA and tax offices are "guaranteed" to be paid in full at foreclosure, regardless of the Investor's loss. If the Seller's financial package indicates they can bring the HOA dues, or Real Estate taxes current, the Investor will include verbiage in their approval letter requiring the Seller to do so. See more negotiating tactics in Chapter Seventeen, *"Short Sale Scenarios"*. Some of the most commonly asked questions are answered.

Once you have the Investor's approval, you are ready for closing! Make sure you read the approval letter closely, and supply copies to the Closer and the Seller. This letter can also be supplied to the Buyer's Agent if they need verification of the approved offer.

NOTES

Chapter Sixteen

CLOSING A SHORT SALE

Closing is where the money is. If you don't make it to the closing table, then you have wasted your own time, and money. By now you should have all the approval letters, and/or letters of "Intent to Release", needed for closing. Now is a good time to get your Short Sale file organized. You will need the approval letter(s), net sheet, listing agreement (with reductions), repair bids, receipts, *Seller's Authorization Form*, Buyer's property inspection, bankruptcy releases (if necessary), death certificate (if necessary), and an executed contract.

Choose a Closing Company with a good track record. There is nothing worse than having the Short Sale fall through at closing because of an inexperienced Closer. Call the Title Company, or Closing Attorney, first to see if they have any Closers with Short Sale experience. This one little call can make the difference between easy money, and a nightmare. You will be surprised at how many Closing Companies now have Closers who specialize in Short Sales. Give the Loss Mitigator the name, phone, and fax number for the Closer you and the Seller choose. The closing will go smoother if the Closer works out the details with the Loss Mitigator directly. Once the Loss Mitigator gets involved, the pressure will be lifted from you for a little while. You may be able to step back, and relax for a bit. But, be sure to check in with the Closer and Loss Mitigator as the closing date nears.

The Loss Mitigator will fax the Investor's approval letter along with closing instructions to the Closer. The Closing Company will use the approval letter just as if it were a payoff. If there is a closing date requirement on the contract, go ahead and schedule the closing. Even if you do not have the Investor's approval letter yet, it will create a sense of urgency. The Loss Mitigator will try to meet the closing date you have scheduled, but, they cannot guarantee *anything* since they must obtain approvals from all liens before closing. This can take a week or so, depending upon how many approvals are needed. As the closing date approaches, and all the approvals have been received, you will probably not hear much from the Loss Mitigator. They haven't forgotten about you. They will be in constant contact with the Closer until the day of closing.

The net sheet you provided when you submitted the offer is what determined the "approved net proceeds" on the approval letter. The Investor will be expecting to receive the *exact* amount at closing. If the net sheet happens to differ from the Closing Company's HUD settlement statement, the net proceeds will differ as well. Now, if the net proceeds from the sale are **more** than the approved net proceeds, you will not need a new approval letter. But, if the net proceeds from the sale are **less** than the approved net proceeds, the Investor will either change the letter, or open up negotiations again. In most cases, if the amount is minimal and/or justified by other factors, the Investor or MI Company will issue a new approval letter with no problem. See Chapter Seventeen "*Short Sale Scenarios*" for special circumstances.

The approval letter from the First lien will specify a closing date, any required contributions from the Seller (cash or note), and the amount of net proceeds they expect to receive at closing. The Closing Company will pull a title, which will uncover any other Secondary liens that have not already been addressed.

If there are enough net proceeds to pay off the First lien in full, the Closer will need to order a payoff from the First's Foreclosure Attorney (if the loan is in foreclosure). A Second lien could then be in a Short Sale position. They will supply an "Intent to Release" letter on their letterhead. This will serve as the approval *and* payoff from the Second. This letter will specify the amount the Second has agreed to receive. This amount will either be whatever is left over after paying the First in full, or a negotiated amount. The letter often stipulates a closing date, too. The Closer will require all liens be addressed with either payoffs, or approval letters for the Short Sale to close.

One thing all the approvals have in common is "THE SELLER MAY NOT RECEIVE ANY FUNDS AT CLOSING". So, if your Seller expects to collect cash at closing, you better set them straight. Any *extra* funds will roll down from one Investor to the other until all the funds have been applied to lien payoffs. The only exception is when the Seller's loan is an FHA. They will pay the Seller an incentive of $750 for a Short Sale closing and another $250, if it closes within 3 months! This is the **ONLY** exception, though.

Occasionally an unknown title issue appears, or the payoff is higher than anticipated, and cause an unexpected Short Sale. You can be caught off guard. These situations can be avoided if you get in on the Short Sale from the very beginning and utilize the *Seller's Questionnaire*. But, if you are being thrown into this Short Sale without warning, then you will appreciate the rest of this book. If the shortage at closing is less than $1,000, the Servicer will be looking to the Agents to make up the difference by reducing their commission. Or, in some cases, they will ask the Seller to contribute with cash, a note, or their FHA incentive to make up the difference. If the loss is too high to reduce with cutting everything to the bone, then you will want to contact the Loss Mitigation Department for assistance. These last minute Short Sales can surprise you, and actually close on time!

Be creative...If the Investor requires a value, supply the Buyer's appraisal. The cost to transfer the appraisal to another company is minimal. If they want financial information on the Seller, fax it to them when completed by the Seller. If they want you to cut closing costs, tell them you have already tried, and are already taking a reduced commission. The Loss Mitigator will consider this an "easy" Short Sale because you are so organized.

The Closer of an Investor approved Short Sale will be required to send a preliminary HUD Settlement Statement to the Loss Mitigator at least 24 hours prior to the closing. The Loss Mitigator will review the HUD to be sure all of the Investor's requirements have been met, and net proceeds are represented accurately. Once the Loss Mitigator approves the preliminary HUD, you are ready to close.

Upon closing, the Loss Mitigator will require the Closer to fax an executed HUD Settlement Statement, copy of the Title Policy, and confirmation of the wired funds. The Loss Mitigator will again check the approved payoff against the wired funds. If they don't match at this point, the Loss Mitigator will refuse the funds, so warn your Closer of this. The Investors prefer funds be wired directly to the Investor's bank account. If there is a settlement to Secondary liens, they will have different instructions on how to deliver their funds. Now it's your payday!

You did it! Each time you complete a Short Sale, you gain invaluable experience. Short Sales can be a lucrative sideline to your current Real Estate Expertise. Review the next chapter for common questions and solutions to your Short Sale problems.

NOTES

Chapter Seventeen

SHORT SALE SCENARIOS

The following are problem and solution scenarios taken from real life experiences. Obviously, not *every* situation can be covered, but the following will give you actual, proven solutions to many Short Sale questions. Although these experiences are derived from Short Sales across the Nation, (including Alaska and the Virgin Islands) you are cautioned to draw upon your own knowledge as a licensed Real Estate Agent for any State restrictions, or requirements. If you are uncertain about what happens in regards to any legal issues, please consult an attorney. Keep in mind; the solutions are from the real experiences of an actual Loss Mitigator, which will prepare you to handle problems arising during your Short Sale listings and offers.

PROBLEM: The Sellers are divorced and one of them is not willing to sign the listing agreement, or any offers.
SOLUTION: Contact the unwilling Seller's Divorce Attorney and explain the benefits of the Short Sale. Most attorneys will agree the Short Sale is the best option for both Sellers. They will be relieved from judgments, tax consequences, and credit damage, in most cases. When one spouse is awarded the home in the divorce, the other spouse typically signs a Quit

Claim Deed, or "QCD". This document takes the name of the Signer off the Title, but does not relieve them from the mortgage debt.

PROBLEM: The divorced Seller living in the property will not agree to move out upon closing.
SOLUTION: If the divorced Seller was awarded the property in the settlement, they do not have to move as long as they keep the mortgage payments current. They will eventually be forced to move out after the foreclosure sale date, which is too late for a Short Sale. Even if they signed a listing agreement; you can lead a horse to water, but you can't make him drink. It is best to clarify this at the time the listing is signed so you do not lose time, or money. You may have to terminate the listing, and move on.

PROBLEM: My Seller is in a rest home, jail, or mental facility.
SOLUTION: In most cases you will need a Power of Attorney (POA) signed by the Seller. This POA will assign a representative over the Seller's financial decisions. Most of the time family members, or attorneys, are assigned on the Seller's behalf. Family members are going to be your best source of information. **True Story:** A Judge actually brought an incarcerated Seller into the courtroom from jail to sign closing documents, all due to the persistence of the Seller's wife.

PROBLEM: My Seller filed a Chapter 13 bankruptcy.
SOLUTION: The solution is basically out of your hands, and in the hands of the court. The listing is put on "hold" until the bankruptcy is either dismissed, or discharged. The foreclosure action is also put on "hold", but only for a period of time. In a Chapter 13, the Seller is put on a court appointed payment plan. The court usually assigns a Trustee to oversee the

plan. In most cases, the mortgage payment is not included in the court's payment plan. As soon as the plan is in place, the Seller is required to start making mortgage payments to the Servicer again. If the Seller does not make payments, or falls behind, the Servicer will ask their attorney to file a Motion for Relief for a "Lift of Stay". If the motion is granted by the courts, the foreclosure will start up right where it was prior to the bankruptcy. Any current offers at the time of bankruptcy filing will be put on "hold" until the court makes a determination of the home's value. If the value is proven to be less than the total payoff, the Trustee will release the home from the bankruptcy and allow it to close as a Short Sale.

PROBLEM: My Seller has filed a Chapter 7 bankruptcy.
SOLUTION: The discharge from the bankruptcy will be required before the Short Sale can be approved by the Investor. Timing is very important since the foreclosure, which is now on "hold", will resume with the Foreclosure Attorney's Motion. The trick is to get the discharge before the Servicer has a chance to foreclose. Offers pending at the time of the bankruptcy filing will be on hold, as well. Again, timing is the key. If the foreclosure sale date was already set when the bankruptcy was filed, once the Lift of Stay is granted, the sale date will be reset very quickly in most cases.

PROBLEM: My Seller is deceased, who will sign the listing and offers?
SOLUTION: If the Seller left a Will which assigns an Executor, they will now be the representative, and sign on the deceased's behalf. If the Will is in probate, work with the Probate Attorney. They are usually very willing to talk about the Short Sale. The Short Sale is a solution for them, too. If there is no probate, a representative can be assigned through the courts.

PROBLEM: The lien holder for a personal loan will not release for *any* amount, but total amount due.

SOLUTION: Have the Seller contact the personal lien holder directly. If they explain their financial hardship, and lack of money *and* equity, the personal lien holder may realize pursuing a judgment would be futile. The Seller should also mention that foreclosure will, most likely, wiped out their lien, leaving the personal lien holder with **nothing**. The personal lien holder may then be more willing to accept less than the total amount owed. Or, they might be willing to let the Seller pay off the personal loan outside the closing. The personal lien holder will have to issue a letter of "Intent to Release" to the Closer before the closing can be completed.

PROBLEM: There is an unpaid IRS tax lien.

SOLUTION: The IRS has been very pro-active on Short Sales for many years. They will require some paperwork (of course), and a value of the property to prove it has no equity, but the IRS will probably release the lien. They retain the right to pursue the Seller outside the closing for any uncollected taxes from the net proceeds. Keep in mind the IRS supersedes all other liens in a foreclosure. Therefore, they will be the first ones paid out of the net proceeds, even before the First lien. The Seller should contact the IRS for the proper forms, and procedures. The delay created by this problem will depend upon which location you call, but it is suggested the Seller apply for this help at the beginning of the listing.

PROBLEM: An unpaid parking ticket or credit card debt has appeared on the Title.

SOLUTION: Once a Short Sale has already been approved by the Investor, these types of liens will most likely have to be cleared up by the Seller. The Investor will not consider changing their approval for further loss on these relatively small amounts owed by the Seller. In some cases, the Seller can work out an agreement on the credit card, pay off tickets, or show proof the liens have been satisfied.

PROBLEM: The offer is high enough to pay off the First lien, but not the Second lien.
SOLUTION: The Seller should call the Loss Mitigation Department of the Second lien. If the First has started a foreclosure, or better yet – a foreclosure sale date has been set, the Second will listen. This is the last thing they want to hear. If the foreclosure sale date has been set, they will be more likely to settle for less, and faster. They need to realize they have a better chance of collecting something now, than at the foreclosure sale. Work with their Loss Mitigators, just as if you were working with the First lien. The approved Short Sale settlement on the Second can be as important as settling with the First. All liens behind the First lien are negotiated separately. If any one of the Secondary liens refuse to settle, the First lien could continue the foreclosure so they can wipe everyone out. If they have to pay too much out of their net proceeds towards other Secondary liens, they will choose to foreclose instead. It is logical, but also deadly to the Short Sale. It could end right then, and there. Poof!

PROBLEM: The Buyers are requiring $2,000 cash at closing for repairs.
SOLUTION: Depending on how high the sales price is over value, the Investor may choose to leave the sales price where it is, and approve the repair allowance. Regardless of this, the Investor will most likely counter out the repair allowance, anyway. If the Buyers reject the counter, try to show proof the sales price is high enough over the value to still be an advantage to the Investor. Another option is to have the Seller check with their Homeowner Insurance. If interior damage was created by something

like a roof leak, the insurance may cover the interior damage created by the roof leak. The insurance claim check will be considered a cash contribution from the Seller. Although the claim check may not cover the entire $2,000 requested by the Buyers, the Investor may be more willing to approve the difference. If you plan to request a reduced sales price to cover the "valid" repair, get 2-3 repair bids. A repair addendum for either the bid amount, or a flat amount can be added to the offer. So, either counter it out, or reduce the sales price, based on the amount of the repair bids The Investor does not want to take any responsibility for the "actual" repair since the property is being sold in an "As-Is" condition. This does not apply to cosmetic repairs.

PROBLEM: The Buyer's Mortgage Company is requiring repairs be completed *prior* to closing. This is most common on FHA/VA loans, or instances where the home may not be insurable for Homeowners Insurance.

SOLUTION: Major repairs are also a concern for the Investor of the home. Since the property will eventually be in their REO Inventory after foreclosure in its *current* condition, the Investor will usually consider either reducing the sales price, or allowing for funds to be held in escrow. These funds would be delivered to the Buyers at closing, who would have the repairs completed *after* closing. Then the Investor would not be responsible in any way for the repairs. Get 2 to 3 bids from a reputable Contractor and present them with the offer. This is strictly reserved for major repairs, not cosmetic repairs.

PROBLEM: The Investor will not approve the repairs, *or* reduce the sales price.

SOLUTION: This creates a real serious snag. You may have to let the

Buyers walk, and get another Buyer who does not require repairs. The Investor will have the final word, unless you can provide logical reasons as to why they should approve it. Think creatively.

PROBLEM: The offer is contingent upon the Buyers selling their home first.

SOLUTION: The Investor does not want to consider any offers with these contingencies, unless the Buyer is already under contract and/or has a closing date set. But, if not, the contingency will either have to be removed, or the Buyer can agree to remain as a backup offer, allowing you to continue marketing.

PROBLEM: The Short Sale offer is Investor approved, but now there are additional closing costs causing the net proceeds to fall below the approved amount.

SOLUTION: Some Investors have a buffer zone for such instances. If the net proceeds fall within the zone, the Loss Mitigator may be able to issue a new approval letter immediately. But, if the Investor does not have a buffer zone, or the amount is higher than allowed, the Loss Mitigator will have to get a new approval letter from the Investor, or MI Company. Many times this scenario occurs at closing, creating a very stressful situation. The very best solution to this problem is to get the Closing Company's pre-settlement HUD statement prior to submitting your offer and net sheet for Investor approval.

PROBLEM: The Short Sale offer is approved, but a pipe busted, and flooded the home before closing.

SOLUTION: First, have the Seller contact their Homeowner's Insurance Company for an estimate of damage, and coverage. All home mortgages *should* have Hazard, or Homeowner's Insurance, in place. If the loan is delinquent, the insurance claim check will be issued to the Seller <u>and</u> the Servicer. The check is then sent to the Servicer, who places the money in the Seller's suspense account. If the home went to foreclosure sale, the funds would be applied towards any loss to the Investor. But, since this home is under contract, the amount of the check to cover the repair can either be deducted from the sales price, or given to the Buyers at closing. The Buyers can then use the money *after* closing to repair the damage. Again, the Investor does not want any responsibility for the repairs.

PROBLEM: The Buyer walked on an Investor Approved Short Sale offer at the last minute.

SOLUTION: If the Buyer walks, for whatever reason, you stand a very good chance of getting the Short Sale approved on the next offer. Once the Investor has opened a file, they want to get it closed. Put the home back on the market immediately. Once a new offer is received, they will be able to compare it to the last offer, which makes the decision quicker.

PROBLEM: The Short Sale offer is approved and a closing date is set up, but the foreclosure sale date is now scheduled to occur before we can close.

SOLUTION: Call the Loss Mitigator who approved the Short Sale, and ask for a foreclosure postponement. The Loss Mitigator will do most of the work in getting the postponement approval from the Investor. Because the Short Sale has already been approved, the Investor has already determined their Savings Over REO. BEWARE: There are some States with specific restrictions creating problems in postponing foreclosure sales. Or, the cost to postpone may out weigh the Investor's benefit of the Short Sale. When you receive approval on the postponement, the Seller should contact the Foreclosure Attorney's office to verify they received the proper notification from the Servicer. Sometimes, there are miscommunications and the attorney does not get the postponement request. The Servicer is usually only able to postpone the foreclosure sale for 30 days, so be sure you have a set closing date. If the postponement is denied, the only way to save the Short Sale closing is to push the closing date up in time to beat the foreclosure sale date. You can close up to the day <u>before</u> the foreclosure sale.

PROBLEM: The Seller is missing. You have an offer, but no Sellers to sign it.
SOLUTIONS: A lot of times this happens when an Investor Buyer wants to make an offer, but the Sellers have moved out, and may be hiding from creditors. No matter who brings the offer to the Loss Mitigator, they will not be able to approve a Short Sale without the participation of the Sellers. This would be a completely dead deal. The Servicer has no other option, but to foreclose as quickly as possible. The only way anyone will be able to purchase the property is either at the foreclosure sale, or after it hits the market as an REO property.

PROBLEM: The Investor or MI Company has asked the Seller to sign a note.
SOLUTION: The Investor and the MI on all liens have the right to ask the Seller to sign an interest free, unsecured, note. The amount and term of the note are negotiable. The Investor will ask for a note when the financial package indicates the Seller can afford to help out with the loss. If the Sellers are employed, and have purchased another home; you can bet on it. Sometimes a note is required due to the type of loan, or the Investor. But, typically, the note is reserved for those who can afford to pay, or have

credit ratings to protect. The Investors note has a rate of return at about 50%, so they don't ask very often.

Chapter Eighteen
SELLER'S SHORT SALE BENEFIT REVIEW

In this chapter, we will review the benefits of the Short Sale for the Seller in depth. It is very important both you, and the Seller, understand these benefits fully. The benefits are your biggest selling point, so be able to explain them in plain language the Seller will comprehend. Don't miss the opportunity to sign a new listing by being too vague, here. The Seller can call the Loss Mitigator to expand on any of these benefits in further detail, or how they relate to their specific loan type.

Forgiveness of debt is a benefit given by the Investor for the Seller's participation in the Short Sale program. If the Seller does not participate in the Short Sale, and lets the home foreclose, they will be liable for the remaining debt. The remaining debt is calculated by the Investor using precise numbers. But, to simplify it for the Seller, you can explain that after subtracting the foreclosure sales bid (bid value placed on the property by the Investor) from the Total Debt (total payoff with all fees applied) the amount remaining is the judgment placed against the Seller (in States permitting deficiencies).

The foreclosure sales bid is determined by two different methods. Some Investors bid at foreclosure based on fair market value, or appraised value of the property. This assures the home does not sell for less than it would sell as an REO. And, some Investors like Fannie Mae typically bid Total Debt at foreclosure, regardless of the appraised value. After years of comparing appraisal values to fair market values, it has been determined that appraisal values, on an average, are approximately 15% higher. Since appraisals set the sales price at origination of the loan, balances are usually comparably higher than fair market value. Thus, you have a Short Sale.

Reasons for the default, commonly referred to as "hardships", must be proven through the information in the financial package. The Loss Mitigator will be reviewing this package before the Seller will be released from a note or cash requirement. Common hardships such as unemployment, illness, bankruptcy, and death are usually not required to sign notes. Hardships which show irresponsibility, or financially "able" Sellers are typically excessive debt (credit cards), divorce, employment transfer, job change, or rental problems. Any of the liens on title can require the note or cash. So, if you have more than one lien, you could chance more than one note requirement.

Notes can be a good alternative for Sellers whose financial hardships are questionable. The Loss Mitigator will pull a credit report and compare the creditors to the financial statement in the financial package. If the Seller has pristine credit, other than the mortgage, or they see another home was purchased, they are prime candidates for the note. It is still worth it to Sellers who wants to preserve their credit, avoid tax consequences, and judgments associated with foreclosure. Of course, most Sellers will not be excited about signing the note, so keep them calm.

Sellers will not be asked for notes if their financial information does not show they have the *ability* to pay a note. The Investor will take the Seller's financial statement and deduct the regular monthly mortgage payment, and then add in a rent payment to determine the Seller's ability to pay. So if you are afraid a note will be requested, look at the financial statement as if you were a Loss Mitigator. You will then be able to prepare the Seller for the possible note requirements, and note options.

The Short Sale benefits still outweigh the note, by far. It's better to pay a small payment each month on an unsecured, interest free note, and avoid continued Collection efforts, judgment, blemished credit, and IRS taxes. If there is evidence the Sellers can afford it, encourage them to either sign the note, or counter back to the Loss Mitigator with more acceptable terms. The Sellers can then move forward with their lives after the Short Sale closing, and leave this embarrassing chapter behind them.

Preserving the Seller's credit is another benefit. The foreclosure notice may already appear on their credit report, impairing the Seller's ability to rent, buy, or sell anything. The Servicer is responsible for reporting the status of the loan monthly, reporting 30, 60 & 90 day late pays. FYI – the payment is not reported as a "late pay" until the Seller is 30 days past due. These late pays can never be removed due to credit bureau legalities. You see, if the late pays were subject to revision, it would jeopardize the integrity of the entire Credit Bureau's system.

The foreclosure notice on the credit report would be removed once the Short Sale has closed and net proceeds have been applied to the mortgage loan account. The Servicer reports final results to the Credit Bureau and replaces the foreclosure notice with other verbiage. After all, the foreclosure never happened, right? Beware, though, Investors or Servicers may require specific verbiage such as "settled for less than owed" or "Pre-Foreclosure", indicating a Short Sale to other creditors. Some Servicers may show the loan as "paid in full", or "closed account" with a zero balance on the credit report, too. It varies from Company to Company. Fannie Mae and Freddie Mac are not specific on this matter and allow the Servicer to report however their Company policies dictates. VA and FHA also leave the verbiage up to the Servicer, who may report the loan as "settled". You saved the Sellers from years of explaining the foreclosure notice to future creditors.

Finally, the benefit which has the most effect on the Seller after a foreclosure is the ***exemption from capital gain taxes***, more commonly referred to as the 1099. This may be one of the most attractive benefits for many Sellers. Fannie Mae and Freddie Mac do not require the Servicer to file the 1099 on "approved" Short Sales. Because of this, once the offer is approved by these Investors, the Seller will be *guaranteed* exemption from the 1099 tax capital gains filing with the IRS. Don't know who the Investor is? Just ask the Loss Mitigator, and you have you're answer to questions on the 1099. Please keep in mind as you review this section, I'm not an Attorney or CPA, but a former Loss Mitigator with many years of experience in Short Sales.

This benefit, or lack of it, can have the greatest impact on the Sellers after foreclosure. Without using all the legal and accounting jargon, the following explanation of the impact of the 1099 is offered from knowledge gained as a Loss Mitigator. The amount of the loss to the Investor is reported to the IRS as a "capital loss", since they were short of a full payoff on the loan. The amount of the loss is considered, therefore, "capital gains" to the Seller. The amount shown on the 1099 will be considered taxable income for the Seller. So, depending upon the amount of the loss, the Seller could find themselves with an IRS lien.

Secondary liens usually do not initiate foreclosure, saving them from legal fees which will most likely never be recovered. They often release their lien for the closing at a set amount of the net proceeds. This amount can be negotiated by the Seller, you, or the Loss Mitigator. It's preferred that the Seller try to talk to them first, and then the Agent. If all else fails, then the Loss Mitigator could step in. Like a 1-2 punch. Since the Loss Mitigator has the final say on the approved amount of the settlement, the Seller and Agent are just warming the Second lien up for final negotiations.

Second liens may approve, pending their right to pursue the Seller for the remaining balance. Sometimes they will ask the Seller to sign an interest free, unsecured, note for a portion of the remaining balance. The Investor or MI Company for the First lien has the same note options. The Sellers can sometimes be placed on a payment plan. On loans owned by the Servicer, or a Private Investor, the filing of the 1099 is strictly at their discretion, but that doesn't mean that it's not still negotiable. You can actually get more creative. Don't give up until the home forecloses. Just keep sending in the offers, whether they want them, or not.

Since the 1099 is a tax issue, you will want to disclaim any knowledge of the tax laws, and refer the Seller to a Tax Attorney, or CPA. If the 1099 is filed, the Seller will receive it around tax time, when they received other forms of taxable income, like W-2's.

However, in California, Minnesota, Mississippi, Montana, North Dakota and West Virginia, where the Investors *cannot* place judgments on owner occupied, un-refinanced home loans, they could file a 1099. This benefit remains the largest benefits for your Seller in those States.

If your Seller is a discharged debtor from a Chapter 7 bankruptcy, they will not be protected from the capital gains, if the Servicer chooses to file the 1099. They have only been discharged from the "debt", not the IRS debt of capital gains. Some attorneys do not wish to jeopardize their clients discharged debt by participating in the Short Sale if a 1099 is to be filed. If a Servicer does not require the filing of the 1099, then there is still a large benefit for the bankrupt Seller, and their attorneys will usually encourage them to participate in the Short Sale program. Be sure to have the Seller discuss this with their Bankruptcy Attorney, and be prepared to answer questions the attorney may have about the process.

Most attorneys are in favor of this program, but it is very important not to talk to Seller's with counsel about the program until you have permission from their attorney to discuss such matters. Sellers who have been discharged from Chapter 7 bankruptcy do not have to supply financial packages. (See Chapter Eleven, *"My Seller Has Filed Bankruptcy"*.)

Check SSQ Consulting Company's Website for the "Seller's Short Sale Handbook". This is an affordable handout to help save you time and money. This handbook describes the process in plain language for Sellers of a Short Sale, and will assist them in preparing their financial package. See the website at ***www.SSQConsulting.com***.

SHORT SALE FORMS

AUTHORIZATION FORM

I, _____, give
             (SELLER)

my real estate Agent, _____
                                    (AGENT)

permission to discuss my mortgage and any information regarding

my listing, including marketing, offers and closing expenses.

_____   _____
SELLER   DATE

_____   _____
SELLER   DATE

SELLER QUESTIONNAIRE

Property Address: _____
_____

_____ _____
Seller Name (full legal)   *Co-Seller Name (full legal)*

Home # _____ *Work #* _____   *Home #* _____ *Work#* _____

_____ _____
Social Security Number   *Social Security Number*

Are there any "other" names on the title?   Yes or No
(If yes, list below)   *(Circle one)*

_____
_____

Are the Sellers divorced? If Yes, attach copy of divorce decree.

Was a quit claim deed signed by any of the Sellers?   Yes or No *(Circle one)*
(If yes, attach recorded copy)

Do you have any judgments or liens against you?   Yes or No *(Circle one)*

Are HOA dues delinquent? Yes or No
If Yes, # of Months _____ $_____ /Mo

Name of Home Owners Association (Give contact name and phone#):

_____

First Mortgage:_____

Delinquent? Yes or No # months? _____ Balance $_____
      (Circle one)

Phone Number:_____ Fax# _____

Account #:_____

Is your mortgage loan in foreclosure?   Yes or No *(Circle one)*

Has Foreclosure SALE DATE been set? Yes or No *(Circle one)*

Date of Foreclosure Sale: _____

Foreclosure Attorney: _____

_____

Second Mortgage: _____

Delinquent? Yes or No # months? _____ Balance $ _____
        (Circle one)

Phone #: _____ Fax# _____

Account #: _____

Third Mortgage, Lien, or Judgment (List all tax liens, personal loans against the home, lines of credit) _____

_____

_____

Contact Names/#'s: _____

_____

Account #s: _____ / _____ / _____

Balances $ _____ / _____ / _____

List reason(s) for the delinquent mortgage payment: *(check all that apply)*

- ☐ Abandonment of Home
- ☐ Fraud
- ☐ Business Failure
- ☐ Casualty Loss
- ☐ Curtailment of Income
- ☐ Death in Family
- ☐ Death of Mortgagor

- ☐ Excessive Obligations
- ☐ Payment Adjustment
- ☐ Illness In Family
- ☐ Illness of Mortgagor
- ☐ Inability to Rent
- ☐ Incarceration
- ☐ Marital Difficulties

- ☐ Unemployment
- ☐ Military Service
- ☐ Payment Dispute
- ☐ Property Problems
- ☐ Title Problems
- ☐ Transferring Property
- ☐ Job Transfer

TYPICAL SERVICER LOSS MITIGATION DOCUMENT REQUIREMENTS

Time is of the essence. We encourage you to complete the enclosed *Financial Statement* form and return it, <u>along with the following information</u>:

1. Hardship letter explaining reason for delinquency.

2. Copy of last two-month's pay stubs

3. Bank statements covering all accounts for the last two months

4. Last two year's tax returns with schedules or W2 forms.

5. Proof of hardship (divorce decree, recorded quit-claim deed, layoff letter, medical bills, etc.).

SELLER FINANCIAL STATEMENT

LOAN# _____

PROPERTY ADDRESS _____

SELLER INFORMATION

| SELLER NAME | DOB | CO-SELLER NAME | DOB |

Seller's Home Address   Co-Seller's Home Address

SOC SECURITY #   HOME #   WORK #   SOC SECURITY #   HOME #   WORK #

OWNER OCCUPIED?   RENTAL?   MONTHLY RENTAL INCOME
  YES OR NO   YES OR NO $
LISTED FOR SALE?   AGENT NAME
  YES OR NO   AGENT PHONE/FAX # _____
ESCROW INCLUDES REAL ESTATE TAXES? Y or N (if No, current or delinquent?)
ESCROW HOMEOWNER INSURANCE? Y or N (if No, current or delinquent?)
BANKRUPTCY?   Chapter 7   Chapter 13   Chapter 11   DATE FILED:
ATTORNEY NAME: _____   PHONE/FAX #: _____

SELLER EMPLOYMENT

SELLER'S EMPLOYER: DATE OF HIRE:
CO-SELLER'S EMPLOYER: DATE OF HIRE:

SELLER INCOME		CO-SELLER INCOME	
Wages (NET)	$	$	
Unemployment Income	$	$	
Child Support/Alimony	$	$	
Disability Income	$	$	
Rental Income	$	$	
Other Income	$	$	

MONTHLY EXPENSES		ASSETS/LIABILITIES	
Other Mortgages	$	Checking Account	$
Auto Loans	$	Savings	$
Auto expense/Insurance	$	Stocks/Bonds/CD	$
Credit Cards/Loans	$	IRA/Keogh Accts	$
Health Insurance	$	401K/ESPO Accts	$
Medical Expenses	$	Home	$
Child Care//Support/ Alimony	$	Other Real Estate	$
Food/Spending Money	$	Cars #1	$
Water/Sewer/Utilities/Phone	$	Car #2	$
Other	$	Other	$
TOTAL	$		$

I agree my Investor may discuss, transfer and share my private mortgage information and personal financial status with real estate brokers, insurers, financial institutions, creditors, and credit bureaus. I understand my Investor will continue any current foreclosure and collection efforts. An alternative to foreclosure must be approved (in writing) by my Investor. The Information contained herein is true and accurate.

Seller Signature   _Date_   _Co-Seller Signature_   _Date_

SELLER'S HARDSHIP LETTER

Mortgage Loan # _____

Property Address _____

I/We, _____ am/are requesting my/our Mortgage Company, Investor, or Mortgage Insurer to review the attached financial statement for consideration of a Pre-Foreclosure Short Sale. I am having difficulty paying my monthly mortgage payments due to the following reason(s):

☐ Abandonment of Property	☐ Excessive Obligation	☐ Military Service
☐ Business Failure	☐ Fraud	☐ Payment Adjustment
☐ Casualty Loss	☐ Illness in Family	☐ Payment Dispute
☐ Curtailment of Income	☐ Illness of Seller	☐ Property Problems
☐ Death in Family	☐ Inability to Rent Property	☐ Title Problems
☐ Death of Seller	☐ Incarceration	☐ Inability to Sell
☐ Employment Transfer	☐ Marital Difficulties	☐ Unemployment

Brief Explanation of Hardship: _____
_____
_____
_____
_____

I believe my situation is Long Term and Permanent. I no longer wish to keep my home, but am unable to sell it for the amount currently owed.

Sincerely,

_____   _____
Seller's Signature   Date

_____   _____
Co-Seller's Signature   Date

GLOSSARY OF TERMS

Alternative to Foreclosure: Options presented to the Seller by the Investor of the mortgage loan. These options include the short sale, as well as modifications, repayment plans and forbearance plans.

Appraisal: A more formal and calculated estimate of fair market value. Appraisals are more commonly utilized at the origination or refinance of the loan, but Fannie Mae requires a full appraisal on all short sales.

Arms Length Transaction: An offer cannot be received from a blood relative of the Seller. The Investor refers to this type of offer as an arms length transaction.

Assumption: An Alternative to Foreclosure option given to family members who desire to keep the home of a deceased Seller. The family members must qualify financially for approval of this option.

BPO or CMA: Broker's Price Opinion or Comparative Market Analysis will include three (3) comparable homes that have sold within the last 6 months and three (3) homes currently listed.

Bankruptcy: A legal action filed by the Seller in an attempt to protect themselves from creditors, including the mortgage.

Breach letter: Letter sent to the Seller after 60 days in default on the loan. This letter is the starting of the referral to foreclosure process.

Capital gains tax: When the Investor has a loss, it is considered a gain for the Seller. The amount of the capital gains is transferred to the Seller via 1099 capital gains. The Seller would be responsible for paying taxes on the amount as if it were income.

Certificate of Attachment: This applies to manufactured homes, or mobile homes, only. The certificate of attachment verifies the land and home structure are permanently affixed. It is very difficult to foreclose on a moving target, so to foreclose successfully, the Foreclosure Attorney may have to obtain this documentation. This can cause a delay, and additional delinquent interest accrual for the Investor.

Closing Company: A Title Company, Escrow Company or Closing Attorney would fall into this category.

Comps: Comparables obtained through the Multiple Listing Service.

Delegated Authority: The Servicer's Loss Mitigator has authority to approve the Investor's Alternatives to Foreclosure options within certain guidelines. This authority gives them the ability to negotiate the terms of the Short Sale without submitting the offer to the Investor for the final approval. Some MI Companies also give certain Servicer's Delegated Authority.

Due Diligence: The process of examining default options to cure the delinquent loans that will a loss for the Investor at foreclosure.

Escrow: The escrow on a mortgage account is paid and monitored by the Servicer. The escrow can include Hazard Insurance premiums, MI Company premiums and Real Estate taxes on the property. Escrow can also refer to funds being held in "escrow" by the Closing Company for the Buyers as part of the Short Sale.

FHA: Federal Housing Association.

Fair Market Value: The marketable sales price based on either a Comparative Market Analysis or an Appraisal. These types of values will take into account other sold properties of comparable condition, style, and size to determine a sales price.

Fannie Mae: Federal National Mortgage Association, one of the two largest Investors in the United States.

For Sale By Owner: Commonly called FSBO listing, these are homes are marketed for sale by the owners, instead of a licensed Real Estate Agent.

Foreclosure: The legal process of taking the home from the homeowner due to non-payment of mortgage.

Foreclosure Bid: The price the Servicer will submit on behalf of the Investor to purchase the property at foreclosure auction.

Foreclosure Sale Date: A date set by the court system, or Sheriff in some states, to sell the home at a foreclosure sales auction. The property will change ownership at the end of the sale and the homeowner will no longer be in title.

Freddie Mac: Federal Housing Loan Mortgage Corporation, one of the two largest Investors in the United States.

HOA Dues: Home Owners Associations sometimes charge monthly for maintenance to common areas and roads. If these dues are delinquent, they can start a foreclosure action. HOA dues that are delinquent must be paid, whether in a short sale or at foreclosure sale.

HUD: US Housing and Urban Development - HUD is the MI Company for FHA loans. They will approve a Short Sale on behalf of the Investor, FHA.

Hardship: The Seller must have an acceptable "hardship" to be approved for a Short Sale. Hardships describe the type of financial reasons for the delinquent, foreclosing, mortgage loan.

Intent to Release Letter: This letter is supplied by Secondary liens who have settle for less than owed on their accounts. The letter must be on letterhead, and be signed and dated, specifying a settlement amount and closing date requirements.

Investor: the Company lending funds for the original mortgage loan for the home.

Life Insurance: Some Sellers have paid premiums for Life Insurance with their escrow payments. Most of these policies will pay off the remaining balance of the mortgage loan. This coverage is sometimes dropped during refinancing.

Loan Modification: Once the homeowner has regained their ability to make a regular monthly payment, they may qualify for this alternative to foreclosure option. The terms of the loan are modified by adding legal fees, delinquent interest, escrows, and typically up to 24 months of delinquent real estate taxes to the principal balance. The interest rate and term of the loan may also be modified, if necessary

Loss Mitigation: A program designed to mitigate or analyze the loss to Investors on mortgage loans.

Loss Mitigator: A person authorized by the Investor to negotiate on their behalf for a variety of default options on a delinquent loan.

Mortgage Broker: the Company that finds a loan for the homeowner.

Mortgage Insurance Company: The Company that insures the loan on losses for the Investor.

Net Sheet: The Agent's estimate of closing costs for the Seller. This is very important since the Investor will use these figures to determine the amount of approved net proceeds they expect at closing.

Outsource Company: A company under contract with the Investor to offer Alternative to Foreclosure options to Sellers of defaulted loans.

Payoff: This term is used in several different ways. The payoff from the Mortgage Company differs from a Short Sale Payoff. The Short Sale payoff is a reduced payoff issued by the Investor of the loan. It is for this reason the clause "Subject to Investor Approval" should be placed in every listing, and offer.

Postponement: Requesting a foreclosure sale date be postponed, or put on hold for a specific period of 30 day increments. An offer must be substantiated with a copy of the executed contract offer, pre-settlement HUD from a closing company, and the Buyer's Investor commitment letter (not pre-approval letter), and faxed to the Loss Mitigator.

Pre-Foreclosure Sale: Another name for the short sale. Pre-foreclosure is the act of selling the property before the foreclosure sale date.

QCD: Quit Claim Deed – which transfers title from an existing title holder to another existing title holder. This is most common in divorces.

REO: "Real Estate Owned". This term refers to the property after it has been foreclosed. The Investor is now the owner of the property and all previous listings are void.

RTC: Resolution Trust Corporation, which was in charge of defaulted loans obtained from defunct savings and loans in the 1980's.

Reaffirm: The bankrupt Seller has an opportunity while in bankruptcy to reaffirm their debt on secured assets they wish to keep. A reaffirmation letter is sent to the creditor by the Bankruptcy Attorney.

Repayment Plan: usually set up by either a collector or Loss Mitigator at the mortgage servicing company. The plans typically are 24 months, or less with a higher payment amount to pay a portion of the delinquency.

Restart State: Georgia and Texas are restart states. The foreclosure cannot be put on hold for a foreclosure postponement. If the Short Sale does not close, the Investor must restart the foreclosure action from the beginning.

Secondary Liens: Any liens other than the First lien. Liens are listed on the title report in the order of their recording dates. These secondary liens can be judgments, tax liens, HOA dues, credit lines, personal loans, or any other types of loans capable of attaching themselves to the Title.

Servicer: The Mortgage Company that "services" the loan for the Investor. This includes receiving payments, paying escrows, collections, foreclosure and Bankruptcy. The Servicer is paid a small percentage as a servicing fee.

Short Sale: The act of selling a home "short" of a full payoff. An Investor Approval Letter is required for closing a Short Sale.

Super Tuesday: Foreclosures in GA and TX have only one foreclosure auction date per month. On the first Tuesday of each month.

Suspense Account: When a loan is in foreclosure, no funds can be applied to the account, or the foreclosure would be invalid. In most States, the foreclosure would have to be restarted. The suspense account is attached to the loan account where funds like Insurance claim checks can be placed without applying them to the loan payments

Third Party Bidders: Those who bids against the Investor at foreclosure.

Total Debt: The payoff of the mortgage loan including all fees. These fees can be foreclosure/bankruptcy legal fees, late fees, inspection fees, NSF fees, payoff fees, and corporate advances, like unpaid real estate taxes or hazard insurance.

VA: Veteran's Association.

INDEX

1099 IRS Filing (See Capital Gains)
Addendum - 81, 82, 108
Agent - 1, 3, 6, 8-9, 11, 13, 15, 23, 29, 31-35, 38-40, 42-47, 49, 51-53, 61, 65, 68, 73-76, 80-83, 87, 91-92, 95, 100, 103, 117, 120, 124
Appraisal – 38, 42, 57, 63, 100, 114
Approval - 3, 13, 16, 23, 28, 35, 57-58, 64-66, 68, 72, 80-82, 86, 95, 99, 106, 110
Approval letter - 8, 19, 40, 58, 64, 66, 68, 84, 86-87, 93-95, 97-99, 109
Arms length Transaction - 85
As-Is condition – 35, 52-53, 81, 108
Asbestos - 84
Asset – 2, 10-11, 30, 47, 75, 77
Assumption – 30, 76-77
Attorney –8, 16, 20-21, 25, 27-29, 31, 36, 61-62, 64, 70-72, 74-76, 97, 99, 103-105, 111, 116-118, 122
Authorization form – 16-17, 33, 36, 64, 97, 120
BPO - 38, 42
Bankruptcy - 5-7, 10, 16-18, 25, 27, 31, 65, 69-74, 97, 104-105, 116, 118
Benefits – 3-4, 12, 15-21, 41, 47, 70, 101, 103, 110, 113, 115-118
Bids – 30, 39, 44, 49-52, 54, 97, 108, 113-114,
Breach letter - 30-31
Breach of Contract - 82
Buyer - 9, 18-19, 35, 40, 44, 46, 50-54, 65, 72, 81-84, 87-89, 91, 95, 97, 100, 107-111
CMA - 38, 42
Capital gains (1099) - 2, 17, 20, 21, 28, 41, 70, 76, 116-118
Certificate of attachment - 44
Closing - 3-4, 6-8, 11, 13, 17-18, 21, 24-25, 29-30, 33, 35, 38, 38, 41, 46, 48, 51-52, 54, 58-59, 62, 64, 66, 68, 71, 74, 76-77, 80, 82-87, 93-100, 104, 106, 108-111, 115, 117
Closing Costs – 34, 40, 42, 48, 62, 79, 81-82, 84, 87, 91, 93, 100, 109, 120
Closing Company – 68, 76, 84, 97-99, 109
Commission – 1-3, 9, 15, 29, 34, 38-40, 42, 46, 48, 74, 79, 89, 91, 100
Comparables (comps) - 42-43, 53
Conflict of interest - 38, 46
Contingencies – 44, 83, 87-89, 91, 109
Cosmetic – 50, 54-55, 83, 87, 108-109
Counter(ing) – 3, 34-35, 41, 45, 55, 59, 67, 72, 80-83, 85-89, 91, 107, 115
Credit Bureau - 17, 19, 115
Credit Report– 2, 11, 16-19, 28, 41, 69, 74, 103, 112, 114-116
Death Certificate - 76-77, 97
Deceased Seller – 17, 30, 75-78, 105
Deficiency - 21, 25-26, 28

Delegated Authority - 6, 65, 67-68, 80
Discharge – 27, 70-71, 73, 104-105, 118
Dismissed - 72-73, 104
Distance - 43, 45
Divorce – 10, 15, 23, 25, 28-29, 103-104, 114, 121, 124
Environmental – 44, 48-49, 51-52, 59, 92
Escrow - 2, 5-7, 11, 53, 63, 65, 94, 108
Equity –1, 24, 30, 41, 48, 57, 63, 76-78, 106
FHA – 1, 3-6, 18, 20-21, 67, 99-100, 108, 116
FSBO or For Sale by Owner- 2, 25, 29
Fannie Mae - 1, 5, 9, 18, 20-21, 42, 114, 116
Financial Package - 16-17, 27, 29-30, 33-34, 37, 41-42, 48, 60-61, 64-65, 67-68, 71, 73, 76-77, 81, 85, 94, 111, 114, 118
Fire Damage - 53-54
Flood – 39, 50, 51, 109
Foreclosure attorney - 25, 27, 31, 36, 61, 71, 99, 105, 111, 122
Foreclosure - 1-12, 17, 19, 21, 23, 25-31, 33, 36, 39, 42, 45, 47-48, 51, 53-54, 58-61, 63-64, 67, 69-74, 76-77, 79-80, 85, 88, 92-94, 99, 104-108, 113-117, 122, 124; (bid) – 113; (sale) - 1, 11, 16, 25, 27, 36, 57-58, 60-62, 67, 69, 88-89, 94, 104-105, 107, 110-111, 122; (pp) - 19, 25, 27, 80, 88, 110
Foundation – 43, 52
Freddie Mac – 1, 5, 18, 20-21, 116
Fuel – 43, 51
HOA – 61
Hardship - 1, 18, 23-24, 37, 41, 106, 114, 123, 124
Hazardous Conditions – 51-54, 83-84
Homeowners/hazard insurance (See Insurance)
Home Warranty Plan - 82
HUD – 6, 19-20, 67, 84, 87, 98, 100, 109
Insurance – (hazard) 5, 11, 63, 110; (life) - 77
Intent to Release Letter – 58, 62, 86, 91, 96-97, 99, 106
Interest (delinquent) - 2, 7, 10-12, 24, 47-48, 65, 73
Investor – 1-13, 15-16, 18-21, 23, 25, 27, 29, 32, 34-35, 37-55, 59, 61-66, 68-71, 73-75, 77, 80-85, 87-89, 91-95, 98-100, 105-117
Investor loss (See Loss)
Judgments – 2, 5, 11, 16, 18, 25, 28, 41, 57, 60, 71, 103, 106, 113-115, 117, 121-122
Late pays – 115
Life Insurance – (See Insurance)
Listing - 1-2, 4, 15, 19, 23-25, 27, 29-30, 33-49, 51, 53, 60-61, 65, 71, 76, 81-85, 97, 103-106, 113, 120
LTV (loan to value) - 63
Loss (potential) - 2-3, 5-8, 10-13, 20, 25, 40-41, 45-46, 48-49, 54, 57-60, 62-68, 71, 74-75, 77, 79-80, 86, 89, 91-94, 100, 107, 110-111, 116-117, 122
Loss Mitigator/Mitigation – 3, 5-8, 10-12, 16-20, 24-25, 27, 30-32, 34-40, 43-47, 49-51, 54-55, 58-62, 64-65, 67-69, 72-74, 77-79-89, 91-93, 97-98, 100, 103, 107, 109-111, 113-117, 124
MLS – 35, 38, 43

Manufactured Homes – 39, 44
Mildew – 39, 43, 51
Mobile Homes – 39, 44
Modification – 2, 9, 23, 45
Mold – 39, 43, 51, 84
Mortgage - 1-5, 7-9, 11-12, 15-16, 19-20, 24, 29-34, 47, 53, 60-61, 71-73, 76-77, 94, 104-105, 108-109, 114-115, 120-122, 124
MI Company – 6, 8, 10, 12-13, 23, 29, 44-46, 59, 63-68, 82, 84-85, 89, 91-92, 98, 109, 111, 117
Negotiations – 20, 26, 39-40, 45, 49, 58-60, 62, 68, 86, 89, 91-92, 98, 117
Net proceeds - 11, 17, 24, 42, 47, 58-59, 66, 79, 84, 86-87, 92, 96-97, 99-100, 106-107, 109, 115, 117
Net Sheet – 60, 62, 65, 81, 84-85, 88, 97-98, 109
Notes - 23, 29, 59, 62, 67-68, 71, 99-100, 111-112, 114-115, 117
Offer – 4-12, 17, 19, 24-27, 29, 31, 35-44, 46-48, 51, 53, 55, 58-62, 64-67, 69-70-72, 74, 76, 79-82, 84-89, 95-96, 103, 105, 107-111, 116-117, 120
Payoff – 1-4, 6, 8, 10-12, 15, 17-18, 23-24, 31, 33-34, 38, 42, 49, 57-58, 62, 66, 72-74, 79-81, 84-85, 92-93, 98-100, 105, 113, 116
Preservation - 12, 48, 83
Private Buyers /Investors – 20, 31, 50, 54, 64, 91, 117
Probate - 75-77, 105
Propane - 51-52, 84
Quit Claim Deed or QCD - 28-29, 104
REO – 1-2, 10, 39-40, 47-51, 59-60, 65, 83, 89, 92-94, 108, 110-111, 114
Recording – 57
Redemption -21, 25-26
Relief, Motion for -71-72, 105
Repairs - 42-44, 48, 50, 52-55, 79, 82-83, 87, 107-110
Repayment plan - 8, 23, 59, 62, 94
Representative - 7, 62, 64, 67, 76-77, 104-105
Roof – 43, 50-51, 53, 84, 108
Second/Secondary Liens – 4-5, 18, 37, 45, 57-63, 66, 68, 79-80, 85, 92-94, 99, 101, 107, 117, 122
Seller's Authorization - 16-17
Seller's Benefits – (See Benefits)
Seller's Net Sheet - (See Net Sheet)
Seller Notes – (See Notes)
Seller's Questionnaire – 4, 17, 24, 33, 79, 99, 121 (Forms)
Servicer - 3, 5-8, 10-13, 16-17, 19-20, 30-31, 34-37, 53, 64-65, 67-68, 70-73, 75-77, 83-85, 89, 94, 100, 105, 110-111, 115-118, 124
Subject to Investor Approval – 35, 81-82, 115
Title – 18-19, 28, 30, 44-45, 57, 59, 76, 84, 93-94, 97, 99-100, 104, 106, 114, 121-122
Trustee - 28, 72, 76, 104-105
VA – 1, 5, 18, 20, 27, 66-67, 71, 108, 116
Value -1-2, 4, 10-12, 25, 29, 34, 38-51, 53-55, 57, 59, 63, 72, 81-84, 91, 93, 100, 105-107, 113-114
Water - 43, 50-51, 84, 93, 104

SSQ CONSULTING COMPANY
P. O. Box 182184
Arlington, Texas 76096

ORDER FORM

NAME: _____
           FIRST   LAST

ADDRESS: _____
             STREET ADDRESS   SUITE #

_____
     CITY   STATE   ZIP CODE

PHONE #: (   ) _____

Title	#	Price
Success in Short Sales @ $19.99 each		$.
Sub Total		$.
Sales Tax @ 8.25%	+	$.
Shipping Charge @ $3.99 each	+	$.
Total Amount Due		$.

Method of Payment

- ☐ Cashier's Check
- ☐ Money Order
- ☐ Visa
- ☐ MasterCard
- ☐ American Express

Credit Card # _____ Exp. date _____

Signature _____